NARCISSISTIC MOTHERS

HOW TO SURVIVE ABUSIVE PARENTAL RELATIONSHIPS CAUSED BY PERSONALITY DISORDERS. RECOVER FROM CHILDHOOD EMOTIONAL CARELESSNESS. A COMPLETE GUIDE TO DISCOVER HOW TO HEAL

HOPE UTARAM

Copyright © 2020 by *Hope Utaram*
- All rights reserved -

The content contained within this book may not be reproduced, duplicated or transmitted without direct written permission from the author or the publisher.

Under no circumstances will any blame or legal responsibility be held against the publisher, or author, for any damages, reparation, or monetary loss due to the information contained within this book. Either directly or indirectly.

Legal Notice:

This book is copyright protected. This book is only for personal use. You cannot amend, distribute, sell, use, quote or paraphrase any part, or the content within this book, without the consent of the author or publisher.

Disclaimer Notice:

Please note the information contained within this document is for educational and entertainment purposes only. All effort has been executed to present accurate, up to date, and reliable, complete information. No warranties of any kind are declared or implied. Readers acknowledge that the author is not engaging in the rendering of legal, financial, medical or professional advice. The content within this book has been derived from various sources. Please consult a licensed professional before attempting any techniques outlined in this book.

By reading this document, the reader agrees that under no circumstances is the author responsible for any losses, direct or indirect, which are incurred as a result of the use of the information contained within this document, including, but not limited to, — errors, omissions, or inaccuracies.

Table of Contents

Introduction 1

Chapter 1 Narcissistic Mothers 3

Chapter 2 Understanding Narcissism 14

Chapter 3 Narcissistic Personality Disorder............. 31

Chapter 4 Characteristics Of Narcissistic Parents 43

Chapter 5 The Future Of Your Relationship............................ 57

Chapter 6 Narcissistic Mothers And Their Sons...................... 62

Chapter 7 How To Deal Withnarcissistic Parents.................... 75

Chapter 8 Recovery.. 82

Chapter 9 Healing From Narcissism 92

Chapter 10 How Manipulations Influence Your Mindset 101

Chapter 11 Therapy 118

Conclusion 122

Introduction

As a girl that grew up with narcissistic parents, especially my mother, I understand that this is a giant burden to overcome. Understanding what a narcissist is and how they work can help you combat the issues that toxic parents can have on us as adults. As we learn how to cope and work through different strategies, it can truly enable us to become better parents when we have our own children.

In this book, I am going to go over what narcissism is and the traits of narcissistic personality disorder. It can manifest in a variety of ways and there are many signs that you are dealing with a narcissistic parent. In addition, I'm going to discuss the effects that this can have on you as the daughter of a narcissistic mother. We are also going to talk about borderline personality disorders and the consequences that come to you when you are raised by narcissistic parents.

There will also be a discussion on emotional intelligence and how it impacts your relationships. Looking over social skills including what they are and how they can help you deal with toxic people or your toxic parents will also be included. I will give you a good foundation on neurolinguistic programming and how it can help you in positive ways.

On top of all of this, we're also going to discuss Cognitive Behavioral Therapy and how it can be used on a daily basis to help change your thought patterns and the way you deal with people. Lastly, the outlook over how you can protect yourself from abuse whether it is mental or emotional. Knowing how to be a wonderful mother and avoid the narcissistic tendencies that you grew up with is probably one of the most beneficial pieces of this book. On that note, let's get started.

Chapter 1

Narcissistic Mothers

Like most mothers, there are many reasons why a narcissistic mother would want to have a child. While they want to love and care for their children, they may also want to have children for all the wrong reasons. They may feel that having children makes them look better in the eyes of other people. Another reason is that it provides them a sense of entitlement. After all, if they are a mother, people should naturally want to help them. Finally, having a child will give them someone who worships the ground they walk on, at least for a few years. However, many narcissistic mothers also wanted to have a child because they always dreamed about it. They feel this is part of their life's mission.

No matter what their reasoning behind their desire to become a mother is, it is important to remember that your mother does love you. You will read a lot of information online that says narcissistic mothers have trouble loving their children. While it looks like this from the outside, the inside of a narcissist is different. The truth is, they love differently because of their narcissism. Until they learn strategies to help control the personality disorder, they will naturally put themselves first. As a child, you should never forget that you are a part of your mother. She cared for you when you were in her womb while you were growing and developing into a soon to be newborn. No matter how the journey has unfolded, there was always love for you in your heart.

No matter how you feel about your mother, one of the biggest steps that you need to take is to recognize that your mother has a diagnosable mental illness. The connections and chemicals in her brain are not the same as they are in your brain. In other words, your mother cannot help that she thinks the way she does. She went through situations in her life which led her to become a narcissist. Of course, knowing this doesn't always make it easier, however it can bring you to a point where you are ready to start forgiving your mother for all the pain and hurt she caused you over the years.

Realizing Narcissistic Personality Disorder is a mental illness is also a big step for someone who suffers from the disorder. Since this book isn't just for children who were raised by a narcissist, but also the person who lives with the disorder, it is important to understand that there is help for everyone. Once you reach the point where you understand that you have a psychological disorder, you can begin to turn your life around. You can start understanding yourself better such as the way you think, why you think this way, and how you can change your method of thinking.

The help that everyone can receive through a therapist is not going to fix everything overnight. It is going to take a lot of time, patience, compassion, and love to overcome the years of damage, pain, and stress that the personality disorder caused. However, the more you work towards creating a better life for yourself, the more you will create a better life for your child. This is something that takes a lot of courage, strength, and is something that you should be proud of.

Signs Of A Narcissistic Mother

There are several signs of a narcissistic mother ("Characteristics of Narcissistic Mothers", n.d.). While I will discuss many of the common characteristics, there is still a lot that will not be mentioned. This is partly because there are dozens of characteristics and partly because everyone is different. While narcissistic mothers will hold some of the same personality traits, there are many other traits which vary from one mother to the next.

Whether you are a mother or child, these signs can be difficult to read. As a mother, you can't imagine you treated your child this way. As a child, it can bring back painful memories. However, in order to overcome the past, you need to recognize the common signs. Not only will this help you further understand Narcissistic Personality Disorder, but it will also help you move toward the future.

She Will Deny Everything

Part of Narcissistic Personality Disorder is placing blame on other people and denying wrongdoing. The biggest reason a narcissist will react this way is because they have a strong need to uphold their best image. Even if people realize they are lying or denying involvement, a narcissist will continue to do whatever necessary to act like they did nothing wrong. As a child, you were often blamed for what your mother did. This is because you were the easiest target to use since you were less likely to argue or speak the truth to avoid receiving her wrath. Furthermore, most children want to protect their parents, just as their parents are supposed to protect them. Even if you didn't receive protection from your mother, you still felt the urge to protect her.

Your Mother Lies to You

Narcissists are known to lie. They do this in order to manipulate or control you to get what they want. They will also lie to themselves. They need to do this in order to make themselves look better in front of other people.

Many narcissists are believed to be compulsive liars, but this isn't necessarily true. Narcissists usually know when they are lying whereas compulsive liars don't always understand they are lying.

It is important to remember that everyone lies at some point in their lives. We also lie for different reasons. While you were often hurt by your mother's lies, it is important to understand this is another part of narcissism. They lie to cover their tracks and avoid looking bad to someone else. They may also lie to try to feel better about themselves. This is especially true for a narcissist who understands their mental disorder and is trying to overcome it.

She Is Manipulative

One of the biggest traits about a narcissist is they are manipulative. A narcissist will use various manipulation tactics in order to gain control of the situation. For example, your mother negatively compares you to one of your siblings, shames or embarrasses you when you don't comply with what she wants or says you are ungrateful and don't care about her.

There are various forms of manipulation ranging from good to bad. A narcissist will rarely use a good form of manipulation such as using manipulation to help someone else hence having an altruistic purpose. For example, when a therapist manipulates you by asking a question in a certain manner, they do so to help you understand yourself better. Negative forms of manipulation are used when someone tries to get you to do something for their own benefit. These are the forms of manipulation your mother will use.

One manipulative tactic is the guilt tripper. There are many examples of guilt trippers. For example, a mother and her son are out discussing whether he should accompany his mother on a shopping trip or go out with his friends. The 13-year-old son tells his mother that he would rather go out with his friends because he can hang out with her at anytime. During the summer, he rarely gets to be with his friends. As he is about to walk out the door, the mother starts using guilt-tripping telling him, "If you really love and care about me, you would spend time with me." Even if the son is starting to understand this is a strategy his mother uses to get her way, he knows that he will feel guilty if he goes with his friends instead of her. He also knows that she will continue to make him feel guilty, even weeks from now about this event. Therefore, he allows his guilt to take over and decides to go shopping with her instead.

If you ever heard your mother use phrases such as "If you knew what I have been through..." or "If you were a good child, you would..." she used guilt-tripping in order to get what she wanted. In reality, she didn't really mean what she said, as manipulators rarely use meaningful tactics to get what they want. She knew this strategy worked on you, so she used it. If you ever stopped listening to her guilt-tripping, then you may have noticed she stopped using it and turned to a different strategy.

Shaming is another form of manipulation which can be used publicly or privately. Today, there are a lot of forms of public shaming thanks to social media. A lot of parents praise other parents who post pictures or videos of their children holding up a sign saying what they did wrong and what their punishment is — this is a form of public shaming. While most of the parents who have done this rarely use this form of discipline, a narcissist will often resort to shaming their child.

Your narcissistic mother might have used the same reasoning to shame you throughout your life or she may have used different reasons. Salem is now 33-years-old and barely talks to her narcissistic mother. She is trying to learn to forgive her mother through therapy but often finds this difficult as she is raising her own two children. As a mother herself, Salem doesn't understand why her mother shamed her so much. This is something Salem could never do to her own daughters. She specifically remembers how her mother would often refer to her as a "bad child" because she was born on a Sunday, which is the day of rest according to God. Salem remembers how her mother would often say, "You already put me through giving birth to you on a Sunday," every time she asked Salem to do something she wouldn't do. She would often use this reason to tell other people how bad her child could be.

Many people refer to public and private shaming as the "Shame Game." Some of the most common reasons narcissistic parents shame their children are to feel superior, weaken self-esteem, gain control, drive someone into self-blaming or self-destruction, manipulate someone into taking responsibility, and isolate them.

The reality about shaming your child is no matter how often you do it, you are emotionally abusing your child. The effects of shaming children in any setting are self-hatred, addiction, self-harm, low to no self-esteem, externalizing or internalizing anger and other negative emotions, fear of intimacy, emotional and physical withdrawal, crippling anxiety, depression, perfectionism, and underachievement.

The self-esteem attack is another form of manipulation. One of the main reasons narcissists use this tactic is to ensure that you believe they are better than you. A narcissist always needs to find a way to keep up their image, whether this is privately or publicly. The most common forms of self-esteem attacks are name-calling, extreme criticism, put-downs, judgments, and labels. Your mother probably said many things to you in order to attack your self-esteem. Some of the most common examples are "Why are you so stupid?" "You will never amount to anything," or "You are worthless." Other types of attacks are not as direct. For example, a narcissistic mother would tell her daughter, "Only girls working the street corner wear those clothes in the daylight."

Another reason that your mother may have attacked your self-esteem was to ensure you wouldn't engage in certain behavior again. For example, if you didn't listen to her, she might have told you that you are "deaf and worthless."

Another form of manipulation is being competitive. Narcissists will turn almost anything into a competition. This can often be a fun game when you are a child, at least until you find yourself losing all the time. One example of this is during the movie Mommie Dearest when the character Joan Crawford, portrayed by Faye Dunnaway, and her young daughter, Christina Crawford, portrayed by Mara Hobel, are swimming in the pool. Joan tells her daughter they should race and she agrees. As the scene unfolds, Joan wins every race against her daughter. Near the end of the scene, Christina gets upset at her mother and tells her that it's not fair she always wins. Joan responds by letting her know she will always win against her because she is bigger and better.

Narcissists will tell their children, "Whoever can do this first, wins!" and always find a way to win. They might even try to be nice by giving you a head start or a warning, but they will still win in the end. If you do end up winning, you will find that your mother becomes irate and might attack your self-esteem in order to gain the upper hand.

The silent treatment is another form of manipulation. This happens when the narcissist withdraws any emotion and forms of communication. For example, a mother who gives her child the silent treatment will ignore them even if they try to ask a question or are in need of something. No matter how often they try to talk to their mother, she will act like she didn't hear them or just walk away.

It's important to note that when she is giving the silent treatment, she is also paying attention to how you are responding. She will pay attention to your facial expressions or gestures as she wants you to feel sadness or fear. She usually wants to see that you are feeling fear of abandonment or rejection. Once you start showing signs of these emotions, she will often start responding to you again. Therefore, one way to end this type of behavior is to disengage and not respond in the way she wants and expects you to respond..

Another type of manipulation is gaslighting or making you feel you're the "crazy one." Before I go any further, I want to say that a narcissist is not "crazy." They have a personality disorder which makes them think a certain way. When a narcissist uses gaslighting as a tactic, they are trying to make you believe they didn't say something, even if you remember them saying it. They will tell you that you said something, which you don't remember saying. They will do this so often that you start to believe they are right and you are wrong. This can make someone feel they are "going crazy."

She Uses Codependency to Control You
There are many children who feel they can never live their own life because their mother is always saying, "I can't live with you so don't leave me." While most parents don't want their

children to grow up and leave them, they know it is inevitable and a part of life. They also feel this is a bittersweet moment as they are proud of their children for accomplishing milestones such as going off to college, getting their first full time job, and buying their own home. Narcissists don't feel the same way. They need their children with them, even if they don't act like it, because it's the only way they can ensure control over you. If you leave their home or move away, they can no longer hold control over you.

She Reacts Extremely When Criticized

No matter who you are or how old you are, you are going to receive criticism from someone now and then. As children get older, they will often start criticizing their parents for various reasons. While most parents handle criticism well, parents who are narcissistic will react in an extreme way. For example, they might punish you, yell at you, harshly criticize or shame you.

Chapter 2

Understanding Narcissism

To understand narcissism, you need to know what it is in itself. Someone who admires their intelligence or their appearance at an extensive level is someone that is narcissistic. They tend to be extremely selfish and have a sense of entitlement that is not warranted. Narcissists typically have a major lack of empathy and they need people to adore them. They will find this adoration by any means necessary.

It is important to note that simply being arrogant or boastful does not make someone a narcissist. It runs much deeper than that. They want to gain control of those around them and be admired at extreme levels, even when it is unjustified. They will abuse those around them to gain this control. Oftentimes, narcissists don't even realize that they have a problem. This makes treating them and changing their outlook extremely difficult.

Regardless of what age you are dealing with a narcissist can be very difficult. It is absolutely the most difficult when you are a child trying to deal with narcissistic parents. In fact, if you are a young child, it is likely that you won't even know what's going on around you just that you are in a bad situation.

Impacts Of A Narcissistic Parent

The impact that narcissistic parents can have on their children is extreme. It can affect the psychological development of the child. This will play a role in their behaviors. In addition, their attitude, emotions, and sense of ethics may be thrown off. The child of a narcissistic parent will have unrealistic expectations that they are trying to meet. This is almost impossible and can completely change how a child deals with the world.

It is important to understand that pleasing a narcissistic parent is almost impossible. Frequently, as a child, this will lead to them feeling as if they are not seen or heard. Their reality will be totally warped. Children that have narcissistic parents are treated as property rather than a person. Obviously, this is going to have major effects on them as they grow and develop.

With these types of toxic parenting skills, many children that are raised in these types of household are not valued as people. Instead, they are praised or criticized based solely on what they are doing. They don't learn how to understand their feelings, and this can lead to terrible self-doubt. As the child of this situation grows up, this self-doubt will play a major role in all of their relationships.

When you are in a situation where you are rated on how you look or how intelligent you are, it is likely that you won't understand or put importance into how you are feeling. It is a vicious cycle that can, unfortunately, turn the child of a narcissistic parent into a narcissist themselves. Being real is not something that will be taught to the child that is dealing with these types of parents. They will believe that their image is exceptionally more important than their true selves.

Keeping secrets is a big part of the narcissist's ways. In turn, the child will be involved in keeping secrets that will keep their family or parent well protected. They will not be able to find themselves, as they will be totally intertwined with what the narcissistic parent wants. There will not be nurturing and, typically, these children will feel emotionally barren. When a child feels this way, it makes it extremely difficult for them to put their trust into other people. This is due to the fact that they understand that they're being manipulated and used by those that are supposed to love them the most.

As parents, we are supposed to be there for our children, however, it happens the opposite way when a parent is a narcissist. This stunts the development of a child in a variety of different ways. Where they should feel loved and accepted for who they are, they will instead feel as if they're being judged and criticized at every corner. This can lead to some major frustration for the child. They will constantly be seeking approval and love but will likely never be able to find it. Not from their parents, at least.

When you are raised in a home where nothing you ever do is good enough, it is obviously going to impact the rest of your life unless you do some work to correct the damage that has been done. Without a role model for good connections with other people, it is very hard to develop these skills. They won't understand what healthy boundaries in a relationship look like. Oftentimes, children that grow up in these types of situations become exceptionally codependent. They don't understand nor do they learn how to take care of themselves emotionally, physically, or mentally.

The child of narcissistic parents will also continuously seek validation. They won't be looking for it within themselves; they will be looking for it from other people. It gets very confusing for these children as they want to do well and make their parents happy, but they absolutely do not want to do so well that they could be looked at as better than their parent. Narcissistic parents tend to get exceptionally jealous of their children when their children do well at something. This will eventually lead the child to a non-understanding of when they actually deserve credit for their good deeds or achievements in life.

Many children that grow up in a household that has one or even two narcissistic parents will suffer from a variety of different disorders. This can include depression, anxiety, and even post-traumatic stress disorder. Oftentimes, this is seen later in life and it can be extremely difficult for them to overcome. There are ways of overcoming the damage that narcissistic parents do, however, it will take a lot of work.

When you grow up in a household that makes you feel that you are unworthy of love, it is, obviously, going to have some major effect on the person that you become. These children are also frequently humiliated by their parents. This leads to terrible self-esteem issues and a sense of shame even when it is unfounded. Sometimes, the child of a narcissist will become an overachiever as they feel they need to be perfect. Sometimes, it goes the exact opposite way. They will simply believe they can't do anything right, even when it is an area they are excellent at. They will tear themselves down and sabotage any chance of succeeding.

Signs Of Someone Having Narcissistic Traits

Many people have narcissistic traits; however, this does not mean that they have a narcissistic personality disorder. Someone with this disorder will consistently be worried that someone around them is better than they are or that they will hold a higher status than they do. It's like they are constantly looking over their shoulders to see if somebody is at their heels. They have a hole inside of them that needs to be filled with admiration or a sense of superiority to those around them. They need people to think they are the best looking or the smartest person around.

There are some cornerstone markings of people that have narcissistic personality disorders. As noted, they will have an extreme lack of empathy for those around them. In addition, they seek admiration on a grand scale. Everything they do is bigger and better than everybody else.

Commonly, people that have narcissistic personality disorder will be described as being manipulative, arrogant, extremely demanding, and self-centered. They live in a world of fantasy and they are convinced that, for some reason or another, they should get special treatment from those that are around them.

Typically, these start to be seen during early adulthood. Those that are labeled as having NPD will show evidence of their disorder in multiple facets of their lives. This includes work, relationships, and parenting, just to name a few.

For someone to be labeled as having a narcissistic personality disorder, they must exhibit several different traits that are commonly seen among people that have this mental illness. The characteristics that you should look for are:

- Self-importance on a large scale
- A desire for excessive admiration
- Unfounded sense of entitlement
- Consistent thoughts of heightened success, intelligence, power, looks, or love

- The thought that they are special and are only understood by others that are special

- Consistent exploitation of those around them

- Severe lack of empathy

- Envious of those around them or the belief that they are envied by others

- High levels of arrogance

There are many other traits that help to pinpoint those with narcissistic personality disorders. They usually do not deal with criticism very well at all. This may be shown with bouts of anger or withdrawing from society. It is surprising that people with NPD tend to fail, considering they are typically higher achievers. With their inability to take criticism and fix their flaws, they are frequent failures in situations like work.

Many people find it surprising that those with narcissistic personality disorders are prone to afflictions like drug abuse and other mood or anxiety issues. It is thought that this is due to the fact that narcissists tend to have impulse control issues. They also experience higher levels of shame that encourage other life-disrupting behaviors.

While these traits are for anyone that has a narcissistic personality disorder, this book is here to discuss the narcissistic mother. Some of the character traits of the narcissistic mother may be quite subtle while others will be in your face. Detecting a narcissistic parent can be difficult, however, it can help you survive what they put you through and allow you to lead a more normal life as an adult.

Many of us don't realize what is happening when we are children, and therefore, we must learn to deal with it as adults. Knowing the signs of what growing up with a narcissistic mother can help heal the emotional and mental damage that they have caused. In addition, it can help to ensure that you do not do the same things to your children and that you are able to build healthy relationships with them.

Most narcissistic mothers have some very defining characteristics. They will often shroud negative thoughts about you in terms that are enduring. They pretend that they are thoughtful when realistically, they are being hostile or aggressive. This is a serious form of manipulation. You may have found that your mother criticized you in a way that looked like she was concerned about you. Showing that she only wants what is good for you by tearing you apart is not an example of good parenting.

Narcissistic parents are fantastic with manipulation. They never come out and say that they don't think that you're good enough, but they will not pay adequate attention when you have done something good. You may find that they're always comparing you to one of your siblings. Noting that your sibling did it better or that you need to work harder to be like them.

Oftentimes, they will simply ignore you or say nothing at all when you share your achievements. By comparing you to those around, it will tear you down and make you feel as if you are lacking in the things that make a person good. This is seriously detrimental to oneself worth. You may find that once in a while your mom says congratulations, but the tone of her voice says something completely different. This is a form of training. It will help to keep you afraid and in line making her the superior of the situation every time.

If your mother is a narcissist, she probably also violates personal boundaries all of the time. You will feel as if you are not your own person but simply a piece of her. There will be a lack of common courtesies. This could look like your things being given away right in front of you. This will be done with no reason and you will simply be expected to accept it.

Frequently, narcissistic mothers will do and say things to try and humiliate you. This can be done by talking about you while you're in the room but acting as if you are not there. In addition, you will have no sense of privacy at home. The narcissistic mother will snoop through all of your things. Even keeping a journal will be impossible. Regardless of where you decide to hide it, you can rest assured that she is going to find it. She will want to know any and everything about you so that she can use it against you in the future.

If you live in a family with several children, the narcissistic mother will likely choose one as her favorite. She will also have one that she picks on more than the others. The favorited child will be granted privileges that the other children simply do not get. They will receive adequate care and encouragement instead of being torn apart for everything that they've done. This child can truly do nothing wrong in the eyes of a narcissistic mother. They are rarely at fault even when they're caught red-handed. She will pass the blame on to other children to ensure that the golden child does not have any black marks.

Unfortunately, the child that is favored over the others will likely become a narcissist themselves. They will become so used to winning and never being in the wrong that the sense of entitlement that narcissists have is bread in them as adults. They will not be able to take accountability and they will feel as if they are superior to those around them. The narcissistic mother has built them up to feel this way.

As horrible as it is, a narcissistic mother is never going to take notice of how well you are doing. That is unless she can somehow take credit for your achievements. If she can't, it will simply be ignored or compared to someone who did it better. As always, she has to be the best. If you are the one that will be gaining attention or adoration, it will be simply, shut down. In addition, she will find ways to hurt you over your achievements. This can be simple little digs with words or major punishments for small inadequacies.

If you are finding joy in the things that you are doing, it is likely that the narcissistic mother is going to try to tear that down as well. She truly does not want you to feel happiness. She will always try to bring you down a notch. This can be done in a variety of ways, but every way that it is done is detrimental to child psyche.

You will frequently see that she criticizes you unnecessarily. This is frequently done by comparing you to your other siblings or the people that are frequently around you. Trying to tell her about the bad things that are happening in your life will be impossible. She will commonly take the side of the person that has done you wrong. This is to help her stay in control. It is a simple way of showing you that nothing you say or do is ever going to be right.

Narcissistic mothers are excellent at making you feel or look insane to those around you. Trying to talk to her about the things she is doing will be shut down immediately. She will blame it on things like your imagination or simply tell you that you have no idea what you are saying. There may be denial even when it was an upfront event. She may outright say that didn't happen or state that she doesn't remember it happening. When this continuously happens, it is likely that you will stop confronting her about issues at hand. This is exactly what she wants.

The envy that comes from your mom will be an intense period if she feels that you have better looks than she does, or you have received something of good quality. Her envy will be easily seen. She may simply take it from you or go and get something better for herself. Narcissistic mothers, as awful as it is, oftentimes, will compete with their children in all aspects.

The lies that will be spouted are also numerous. At any given point, you can place bets on the fact that she is likely lying about a situation. Lies are excellent for creating conflict. This is also a good way to gain control. Narcissists are careful with their lies and become extremely good at it. They will spin stories to make themselves right not only to you but all that is around you. She will use words that will allow the lies to go to the wayside if she is specifically caught. There will be no outright acceptance of the fact that she is told a lie, instead, she will use words like "maybe" or "I guess".

As noted, manipulation is one of the favorite choices for a narcissistic parent. This can be done in a variety of ways, but it starts very early in life. You will find that it is to pinpoint their manipulation tactics. This is very unfortunate since manipulation is a major issue with many adults. It is extremely selfish and will be used against you as long as it possibly can be.

Narcissistic mothers tend to be extremely self-absorbed. They are also defensive towards any sort of criticism that may be thrown their way. It can often be shown by an explosion of emotions after being criticized. She will terrorize you for trying to show her that she isn't perfect.

Unfortunately, there is no true cause found for those with narcissistic personality disorders. It develops like other mental health issues. It is likely a complex set of circumstances that leads a person to act this way. Many believe that the environment you are in plays a major role in this disorder. If you grew up in a house with a narcissistic mother, you are more likely to become one yourself. This is especially true if you don't take the time to recognize what is going on around you.

Others believe that it is simply genetic that we inherit these traits and that it is unavoidable without serious work. There are also thoughts that the way our brains are wired could be the link as to why this happens. The way we behave and the way we think definitely play a role in who we are. So, if you are attuned to the traits of a narcissist, it can be easier to develop a narcissistic personality disorder

We commonly see this disorder cropping up in teenagers and those that are entering into adulthood. We may see signs of it in children, however, these typically don't manifest into anything more once the child develops socially and emotionally. This is, unless, the child is growing up around other narcissists and learns that the behaviors of their parents are acceptable.

There are a variety of signs that you may be dealing with a narcissistic mother. Through their behaviors and their parenting style, it can be easy to pinpoint. Once you have the ability to see these things about your mother, it can make it easier to cope with. It can provide you with an understanding of what is going on and help you combat the effects of it. Obviously, common knowledge is power and when you are dealing with a narcissist, it can help ensure that you do not become the same.

One major sign that you are dealing with a narcissistic parent is that they try to live through their child. For the most part, parents wish that their children are going to succeed. The narcissistic mother, however, will have a set of expectations that will benefit their own desires rather than those of their children. They will want their kids to accommodate their personal desires while putting their own on the back burner.

If you find that your mom is frequently threatened by your successes, it is also a sign that they have narcissistic tendencies. Their own self-esteem will be impacted negatively when you do well. When this happens, it is likely that they're going to tear their child down. This will allow them to stay the superior person in the relationship. This can be seen with massive judgment on the child, comparison to others that did it better, rejection of accomplishments, and simply nitpicking.

Another sign that your mother may be a narcissist is a huge self-image. They may be extremely conceited about who they are. Frequently, they do not treat those around them very well nor do they treat them as you would other human beings. They simply see people as ways to achieve personal gain. They will even go to the extent of destroying those around them if it means that they will get what they desire.

The narcissistic mother will try to ensure that everyone around them understands how unique and special they truly are. This is typically misguided and unrealistic. It may be that they believe they are the most beautiful, smartest, or own the best things and they want everyone to know it. They need the attention that will help to boost their ego. They have an attitude that says, "look at me and what I can do".

Manipulation is a major component in the narcissistic mother's arsenal. They are excellent at using the guilt trip to their advantage. Blaming you or shaming you for what has happened is also extremely common. These types of manipulation can be difficult to wrap your mind around. Other ways that they will try and manipulate you is by using comparison. Asking you questions like, "Why aren't you as good of a student as your sibling?" is one prime example. It is common for them to offer love as a reward rather than something that you deserve. They also, conversely, threaten to take away love as a form of punishment.

Narcissistic parents frequently have strict expectations for their children. They focus on the small details and if there is any misstep, they make a huge deal out of it. This can truly impact a child's way of thinking in self-esteem. These parents are also very touchy. They can be set off very easily and tend to become irritated at the drop of a hat. This is all due to the fact that they want total control over their child. They will not react in a typical fashion, instead, they will blow up at the smallest of things.

Possessiveness and jealousy are also pretty good signs that you are dealing with a narcissistic mother. Due to the fact that they want total control over a child's life, they may become jealous at milestones of maturity or independence within their child. This shows them that there is separation and they do not handle it very well at all. They may make you feel guilty for doing well and moving on in life. They want to know that you are always there for them and that you are wrapped around their finger.

These are all a good look at the characteristics and actions of a narcissistic parent. However, you should be aware that there are many other symptoms or signs that you are dealing with a narcissist. Keeping yourself protected and understanding how your parent is treating you is not always easy. When you know what to look for, it can become easier. This will help to ensure that you lead a healthy and prosperous life as an adult and that you get out from underneath the thumb of your narcissistic mother.

Chapter 3

Narcissistic Personality Disorder

Most experts in the field of psychiatry believe that Narcissistic Personality Disorder (NPD) cannot be cured. This means that people diagnosed with it will have the symptoms of the disorder all their lives and will have to continually work hard to deal with the behavioral difficulties caused by the disorder.

Although people diagnosed with NPD might experience relief of symptoms and might learn valuable coping strategies, they will still have some signs of the disorder for the rest of their lives. Also, most psychiatrists don't believe that medication works well to control any personality disorder, especially NPD.

Narcissism is a kind of belief a person has about themselves, that they are unique and more important than others around them. With this belief, they often act in particular ways and will do things to boost their image in the eyes of others.

The belief in their superiority over others is so deeply ingrained in narcissists that they experience many difficulties when dealing with other people as they will often treat everyone else as less important.

Narcissistic Personality Disorder (NPD), therefore, is the term that connotes a type of mental disorder wherein the individual affected has an exaggerated sense of self-importance.

Individuals affected with NPD have a deep need for reverence from others, though they lack empathy for others. Individuals affected with NPD do not present themselves for psychological treatment because they do not see that there is an issue with their conduct, even though they are aware that people around them constantly find them very difficult to deal with.

The criteria officially used for diagnosing Narcissistic Personality Disorder are described in the Diagnostic and Statistical Manual, Version Five (DSM-V). The DSM-V is the book mental health experts use to diagnose mental illnesses.

It is pertinent to note that some people might display signs of narcissistic tendencies but do not have full-blown NPD.

A few criteria for diagnosing NPD as described in the DSM-V are:

A. Antagonism, characterized by Grandiosity, and

B. Attention seeking.

The criteria described in the DSM-V can be explained through the actions of the particular individual suffering from NPD. An individual who is affected by NPD will only think of themselves.

Their actions will reveal that they think only about themselves and seek to put down individuals around them.

For instance, an individual suffering from NPD may misrepresent their contribution to a work project while deprecating the commitment of a co-worker to the project. The individual might even steal the ideas of others and take credit for the ideas and actions of others. An individual suffering from NPD must be at the center of the universe at all times.

To be diagnosed with full-blown NPD means that a person must exhibit this attention-seeking behavior both over time and in many different circumstances. They must have exhibited it as a young adult, and they must have grown older without much change in their behavior. They exhibit attention-seeking with their family, at work, and in the community. This personality trait seems stable, no matter who they are with and what they are doing.

A person suffering from NPD cannot have their behaviors explained based upon how old they are. For example, many teenagers act like they are the center of the universe and may exaggerate their actions, but this can be explained as a normal stage in their psychological growth, which they will eventually outgrow. However, a person with NPD will never abandon their teenage behaviors. So for an adult, some acts are not considered normal. This is one of the reasons why personality disorders such as NPD are not diagnosed until a person is an adult.

Someone with NPD will seek attention and have a false sense of self no matter what their state of sobriety is. For instance, a person who behaves like a narcissist while drunk, but is a loving and healthy person while sober, would not be diagnosed with NPD because their behaviors are as a result of the alcohol in their system. Someone with NPD will act like a narcissist no matter what their state is.

Taken as a whole, when someone has NPD, they believe that they are the center of the universe and everything revolves around them and as such, they bear no regard for the feelings of people around them, along with the fact that they will not be empathetic with other people.

People suffering from NPD will do whatever they can to be the center of attention and show others how significant they are to the world. They will continue to show these traits throughout their whole lives. Usually, these traits start to show in their lives during adolescence, and they will carry these traits into adulthood.

It is estimated that up to 6.2% of the general population suffer narcissistic personality disorder and that men are more than twice as likely to be diagnosed as women.

How Narcissistic Personality Disorder Develops

As with any other mental illness or personality disorder, there are different explanations for NPD. The causes of NPD could show up independently or exist along with one another in someone's life; this will then encourage the development of NPD.

The first puzzle piece in the development of NPD is genetics. If a family member had NPD, it is quite likely that children and some other relatives might also develop the disorder. This is because of psychobiology; the idea that the brain and human behaviors are connected. If the brain is genetically wired in one way because of the genes a person has inherited from parents and grandparents, then a person is likely to inherit the genes that caused for the wiring to occur in such a way to create NPD. People who have a genetic predisposition are more likely to suffer from NPD than those without it.

The other trigger for NPD is parenting issues. If a person lives with a parent or in a family situation where they are overly pampered, treated continuously as unique, or given everything they ever ask for without any idea that there are limits, they are more likely to develop NPD. Children need boundaries and discipline, and without them, they will grow up with an unrealistic view of both themselves and how the world works. They incorporate the belief that they are special and perfect into their worldview.

On the other hand, people who grew up with parents who were especially harsh and never valued anything the child did can also develop NPD. The child develops a defense mechanism to offset the negative and constant criticism that they receive. Think of it like a pendulum swinging the other way. If the parent is overly harsh to the child, the child will start to overcompensate by believing that they are entitled to everything, that they are special, and that they deserve the world, just to combat the negativity that surrounds them every single day. This is generally thought to happen because the child may be overcompensating to try to prove their worth to their parent. They want to earn the parent's love and approval.

No matter which type of parent the person with NPD had, the parental behaviors began while the child was young, generally before the age of three.

A third factor that may be relevant to the development of NPD is society's ideas of who and what is important. For example, the idea that the most powerful, rich, and successful are more important than "ordinary people" has become an ingrained belief thanks to mass media's preoccupation with these types of people. In watching reality TV, people who are self-centered, selfish, and rude to others are idealized, whereas people who are caring and compassionate are often marginalized or completely ignored. Second, people receive more approval from outside influence when they are smarter, more prosperous, or have a higher status. This could cause people to work for this higher status so they can receive the same type of recognition. Last, there is a weakening of the community in our society.

Children are not often brought up to believe they are part of something bigger than themselves, which leads to kids having more difficulty identifying with others. A grandiose self-image replaces their ability to empathize.

Usually, however, there is a mixture of both genetic factors and environmental factors, both personal and societal, at work with the development of any personality disorder. If a parent or other close family member has the personality disorder, the child will likely grow up both with a genetic link to get it and in an unstable home environment where the traits are more likely to develop. Because many of the traits have been shown to exist since childhood, it is easy to see why the disorder becomes so challenging to treat.

However, that doesn't mean there are not treatments or options for a person suffering from NPD or their families.

You will, undoubtedly, have heard of the term 'Ego'. It is naturally assumed that everyone has one; although some people's egos are much larger than others. Ego is an idea of your self-worth; in many people, this is a fragile item; easily affected by others and their opinions and views.

Your ego will be built upon your own beliefs and experiences throughout life; if you have always met with success, you are likely to have a bigger ego and be more confident. Likewise, those who often meet with failure will tend to have a diminished ego and be less confident in their abilities.

Everything you undertake in life will help to build or diminish this ego; it is a moving, almost living thing, and this is an essential, healthy part of life.

Egoism is an extension of this principle; it believes that all actions and goals should relate to yourself; everything that you do should benefit you and help you to reach your own goals. Moving a stage past this and you become someone with NPD; when the achievement of your goals and the benefit of your actions focuses entirely on you. This should be regardless of the effect on those around you. Egoism is often disguised as kindness and generosity; giving someone else a gift without a reward can seem selfless; in fact, it is often a tool used by someone with NPD to manipulate and gain the support of others; the gift can later be mentioned to ensure a favor is provided when needed. A true egotist will not consider the thoughts of others; their interests lie only in what is good for them.

An ego which centers on your own needs above all others is essential for the creation of NPD. What is perhaps the most interesting thing about this is that it is agreed that someone is born without any ego. At the moment you are born, you do not have any preconceived ideas about the world, yourself, or even any knowledge. All these things are built upon from the moment you are born. Your first instincts will be to reach out and explore the world around you; in a baby, this is done through the senses; sight, touch, smell; hearing, and taste. At this point your ego is simply a reflection of what others think and do; if they praise you and smile at you then you will feel good about yourself, if they do not, you will feel bad about yourself. From this simple beginning, your ego will grow and will be fed by the images and experiences around you. From this standpoint, an egotist or someone likely to have a narcissistic personality is a product of society. Of course, this is a very simplistic approach as there are many other factors which will influence the development of NPD; the exact cause is not known but could be linked to your genes.

The definition of egoism is that the self-belief created by your ego is essential to ensuring you make the correct moral decisions and, therefore, behave by accepted moral standards.

Of course, these standards also extend to assist in understanding the development of NPD; egoism accepts that anyone should put themselves first and this self-belief should motivate all conscious actions; this means that self-interest is an acceptable conclusion to any action, which is exactly what someone with NPD does!

Selfishness is also a trait of someone with NPD; their desires are placed above all others. They see themselves as more important and worthy of success than anyone else, and this becomes a justification for being selfish. Almost everyone has been selfish at some point or the other in their life; it could be hanging onto a vital person because they need them rather than it being the best thing for the person or the relationship. Alternatively, it could be something more straightforward, like taking the last chocolate!

However, the traits of selfishness are sometimes essential in parts of life. Business leaders, in particular, need to put the interests of their company first to succeed. This can even be seen to be essential for preserving the jobs and welfare of their employees. However, putting the company's needs first will also ensure that their own needs are being given priority. The very traits which are essential for business success can start someone on the course to a narcissistic personality even if they do not develop NPD.

The economic acceptance of selfishness as an essential trait if the business shows the complications which arise when trying to establish the parameters and definition of someone suffering from NPD; in many walks of life their behavior will be akin with an extremely successful person. By this logic, selfishness is a desirable and even essential trait for those who wish to succeed.

To be genuinely selfish you need to be devoid of empathy or consideration for other people's feelings; this is, perhaps, the critical point at which someone will change from being considered socially 'normal' and having a personality disorder. Anyone who has NPD will be unable to establish empathy with those around them; this inevitably leads to the ability and desire to manipulate those around you as you lose the ability to respect their feelings or needs. This type of behavior is associated with those suffering from NPD as well as psychopaths.

It must be understood that, as with all personality traits, it is essential to have an awareness of self and to look out for your interests. Being selfish is necessary at times to ensure you stick to your principles, values, or simply to complete a job close to your heart. The crucial difference is understanding the effect this may have on others and choosing to do it anyway, despite the emotional and physical consequences. If you are never selfish, you will never stand up for anything you believe in and will be likely to spend your life following the herd, possibly never achieving your full potential.

It has been suggested that selfishness in adults can be created through a difficult childhood. Any child who has little or no praise or even acknowledgment of their existence is likely to retreat into their world. Some of these children will become recluses and socially inept for life; others will build their fantasy worlds to retreat into and escape the harshness of their life. These fantasy worlds will often revolve around having the control, power, and admiration that they are not receiving as a child. These worlds can be carried into adulthood, and a narcissistic personality will develop as the desire to be appreciated will eclipse all other feelings. Again, this development will be in conjunction with other influences and your genes.

Selfishness is a trait of someone with NPD; however, you can be selfish without having NPD. Aside from the healthy form of selfishness which has already been discussed; most people find themselves being selfish because of the demands and stresses of their own lives; it is not a fundamental desire to hurt others but rather a reaction to your environment. Selfish people tend to come across as selfish, while people with NPD are charming and will appear to fit in well, while being very accommodating. This is because they are manipulating and controlling people around them to obtain their own selfish needs. The difference in personality is both easy to spot and an essential part of the difference between someone who has NPD and someone who does not. After all, someone who truly has NPD will be very concerned with looking good to others; this will ensure they get the help they need to achieve their goals. They will appear trustworthy and unselfish when, in fact, they are the exact opposite; the problem is their charm and charisma will hide their true personality and motivation from you.

Chapter 4

Characteristics Of Narcissistic Parents

Mothers are the foundation for their children's attachment to the world. We all tend to learn from our mothers based on the mode she shields and protect us from harm, nurture us, and cares for us. The potential of a mother to meet our basic needs, validate our pain, tune to our emotions, and provide us with a healthy attachment has a significant impact towards our emotional regulation, attachment styles, and our development. However, this is not the same case for those brought up by a narcissistic mother. One of the major sign about narcissist mother is that they taught you to believe that you are an imbalanced and a crazy one; subjecting to endless doubts about yourself and any feelings that you have about them. The other sign is the constant guilt that never goes away. You realize that maybe something is wrong with your mother but you feel ashamed to even think that way and beat yourself instead. The following are the most common characteristics of a narcissistic mother:

• Everything she does is deniable. She presents selfish manipulations as gifts. She is hostile and aggressive but she presents her actions as acts of thoughtfulness. She fulfills her cruelties with loving terms and she always gives excuses and explanations. For her, all she wants is the best for you, to help you. She will never admit that she thinks you are inadequate but instead, when you tell her you have done something wrong, she counters you with something that was done better by your sibling or just respond with silence. However, she will eventually do something cruel to you to teach you a lesson and ensure you don't get above yourself. She accurately separate cause (the joy in your achievements) from effect (denying you to attend the awards ceremony) in a manner that someone who doesn't live in the abuse will never understand.

She uses comparison as her major putdowns. She keeps talking about how someone else did something wonderful on the same thing you did and the contrast is aimed up to you. She ensures that you are no good without even saying a word and spoil your pleasure by congratulating you in an unhappy, envious, and angry voice making you feel useless. She is completely deniable. Even though it is always possible to confront someone by observing their facial expressions, the way they look at you and their tone of voice, the case for a narcissistic mother is different. She makes sure you fully understand the punishment that will follow immediately if you object any of her opinions which makes you afraid, feeling that you are always wrong, but you can't point out why.

Since her abusiveness is long term and you are always her daughter, you will always find it hard to explain to other people why she is bad. She is always very careful about how she engages her abuses and she is always very secretive. She always makes the right timing for her abusive actions to ensure that no one will hear or notice her abusive behaviors. However, to the public, she emerges as completely different and she will always handle you with concern, love, and understanding. As a result, narcissists usually reports that no one ever believes in them. In other cases, therapists end up siding with the narcissist mother leaving the child isolated and helpless.

• She violates your boundaries. You constantly feel like you are an extension of her. She always gives out your property without even asking, sometimes even in front of you and when you complain, she will confront you that it was never even yours. She expresses opinions that were meant to be yours and commit your time without even consulting you. She discusses you while present as if you are not there. She doesn't respect your privacy; she storms into your bedroom or bathroom with or without your consent. She keeps asking nosy questions, snoops into your conversations, diary, letters, and email. She is always digging into your feelings, especially if they are negative and can be used against you. She is always against your wishes without feeling embarrassment or thought. Every attempt at your past autonomy is strongly resisted while normal rites of passage such as dating, wearing makeup, and learning to shave are allowed after strongly insisting and if you try to resist, you are heavily punished. For example, she can say that "since you have grown enough to date, you can as well start paying for your own clothes." If you try asking for age-appropriate rights, control over your own life, grooming or even clothing, then you are considered arrogant and she ridicules your independence.

- A narcissistic mother also has a favorite. She selects one child, or even more, to be her golden child and the other one, or even more, to be her scapegoat. She offers her golden child with all the privileges as long as he/she follows her instructions and does what she wants. She has expectations that the golden child should be respected by everyone in the family while the scapegoat role is to care for the mom. The golden child will never do something wrong unless it's against her mother's will. However, the scapegoat is always at fault which creates divisions among the children where some consider the mom being wonderful and wise while the rest finds her being hateful. The narcissistic mother fosters the division by lying with blatantly unfair behavior. The golden child takes an active role to defend her mother and perpetuate the abuse indirectly by finding reasons to blame the scapegoat in place of the mother. The golden child aids the narcissist mother with her abuses towards the scapegoat ensuring that she doesn't do it just by herself.

- A narcissistic mother also undermines. She can only acknowledge the accomplishments of her children if she is capable of taking credit for them. However, if they don't benefit her, she diminishes or ignores all the accomplishments or success. Whenever you are at the stage and she can't get a chance to be the center of attention, she responds negatively by trying to prevent the occasion altogether; she misses the event, she leaves the occasion early, she acts as if it is not a big deal, or even leave a negative comment that someone else did better than you even did. She even creates unnecessary fights to undermine you and makes you feel unpleasant just when you are about to make a major move. She will often withdraw her efforts and attention whenever you have opportunities she doesn't like and refuse to do even the very little things to support you. She acts nasty towards things you find joyful and those that are connected to your success which makes you feel useless even if she does not directly say it. She always makes sure that regardless of the efforts you are putting towards your success, she takes you down to peg for it.

• She always denigrates, criticizes, and demeans: A narcissistic mother makes sure that you are aware of all the little things. She thinks less of you as compared to what she does to other people or your siblings in general. If in any case, you complain about mistreatment by someone else, she immediately takes the other person's position to attack you even if she knows nothing about the other person. She never acknowledges your complaints or about those people's justices. All she cares is to make you feel that you are never right. Often, she will say some generalized barbs that are often hard to rebut. For example,

"No one could ever put up with the things you do," "you are always a trouble maker," "you are very hard to live with," "you never finish anything you start," "you are difficult to love," "you are always difficult." However, she always complains about herself in a sidelong way. You will hear her complain that everyone is so selfish, no one cares, loves, or do anything for her while you are the only person in the room. This is a combination of criticism and deniability.

Additionally, she will always compliment something they did with someone else; something you participated too, showing you that she didn't like it about you. She will always try to show you how her relationship with other people is wonderful in a way that will make you realize that it is not the same between you two. In this case, the silent message she is trying to communicate is that you don't really matter to her. She ignores discounts and minimizes your opinions and experiences. She meets your insights with accusations, denials, and condescension. For example, while studying, she will ironically say, "I think you read too much." Additionally, she will brush off on whatever you say even on those fields you are acknowledged as an expert. She confronts you with smirks and abused sounding or some exaggerated exclamations and ensures she doesn't listen or do whatever you say.

- She ensures you look crazy. If in any case, you try to encounter her about something she has done, she insults you telling you that you have a vivid imagination. This is common across all sorts of narcissists to invalidate your experience over your abuse. She also abuses you that she can't understand what you are talking about. She pretends to forget about very memorable events denying like it never happened, and when you remind her, she does not admit of any possibility that she might have forgotten. This tactic is referred to as "gas-lighting," and entails a very aggressive and exceptionally infuriating behavior that is common across all sorts of narcissists. She undermines your perceptions of reality which kills your confidence in your reasoning power, your memory, and intuition which makes you a complete victim to her. Moreover, narcissistic mothers are always gaslight. You will hear them telling you that you are unstable to listen to some certain things. They refer to you as over-reactive, completely unreasonable, hysterical, always imagining, or oversensitive.

Once she has constructed these false fantasies of your emotional pathologies, she will share them with others showing them how helpless and a victim she is with you around her. She always claims to be innocent and states that she completely doesn't understand why you are so angry with her. In fact, you end up being the one who hurt her and thinks that you need psychotherapy. She claims how much she loves and care about you and would do anything to see you happy but she doesn't understand how. According to her, all you do is pushing her when all she wanted was to help you. She complains that she has sacrificed her responsibilities for your empathy and concludes that something is really wrong about you. She uses this as a weapon to undermine your credibility with her listeners by clearly elaborating how perfect she plays her role as a mother.

• A narcissist mother is also envious. Whenever you get something right, she gets envious and angry which only disappears if she loves whatever it is that makes you successful. If not, she will make attempts to spoil it for you, take it from you or get the same but better for herself. She always makes sure that she is on the right track to get what other people have. Narcissistic mothers envy goes way far to even competing sexually with their daughters or daughters-in-law. They are actively forbidding them to groom themselves or even wear make-up while also criticizing their looks. The envy can also extend to relationships where the narcissist mother interferes with their children's marriage and the upbringing of their grandchildren.

• A narcissist mother lies in numerous ways to coun. Whenever she is talking about something that has some emotional significance to her, it's fair to say that she is lying. It is the only tactic she uses to create a conflict in relationships and between those people she lives with. She lies about her feelings, what they have done, and what other people have said about them. She lies about the relationship between you two, your situation, or even your behavior to make sure that your credibility is always undermined. However, she is always cautious about how and when she lies. To the outsiders, she does so in a deliberate and thoughtful manner that can be covered if confronted. She changes whatever you said to take a negative meaning by putting some dishonest interpretations about what you did. When she engages in something bad, she uses preventive lying and speaks before you say anything. When you finally speak, she confronts you with phrases like, "I already knew it." Since she is always very careful with her lies, you might never realize it.

When she is lying to you, she does so blatantly. She will pretend not to remember the bad things she has done. She lies openly even if what she did was so recent or it's something impossible to forget. When you give in with the lie and tries to make her remember about the issue, then she refers to you as having a "vivid imagination." She will confront you with questions like, "why do you hold onto grudges?" Your conversions are always full of brush offs where she makes you feel useless. She doesn't respect you and at the end of the conversation, she makes it not sound good. Your conversations are only based on one rule; you will never win. She only acknowledges she is wrong on very rare occasions and when she does, she admits deniably. For example, she uses phrases like "might have," "she guesses," "maybe" she has done something wrong. She always trims the wrong action to make it sound good. She uses the phrases out of guilt because she knows very well what she did.

• She wants to be the center of attention all the time: Children are the source for adoration and attention for narcissistic mothers. More often, you find yourself doing some chores in the most appropriate time just because she sees you there. You find that something you didn't have to do that day or that week you have to do it on her demand. She creates outdated occasions just to be at the center of attention such as the memorial of someone who died a long time ago. She opts to be the entertainer so that she can be the life of her own party and will make attempts to distract or spoil when someone else drags the attention especially if it's the moment of her scapegoat child. She always invites herself during moments when she is not welcome. When either of you pay a visit, she requires you to spend the time with her and entertaining her is endless. When you happen to do something without involving her, deprived her attention, or refused to wait for her on something, she ends up being raged, manipulated, or even pouted.

Furthermore, older narcissistic mothers use aging natural limitations like doing things that will make them ill as an advantage. For example, if she is deprived of some foods by the doctor, she will intentionally take them to get ill and hence, drag the attention. When they fall ill, they use all the means they can get to you and demand immediate attention and hence, attendance. She expects you to weep over her pain, pat her hand, rush to her side, and listen sympathetically to her endless pain and how awful it is. This doesn't make you any better though; she subjects you to difficult conditions that could have otherwise been avoided. However, if you fail to give her the attention and the audience she is manipulating, she makes you look bad to everyone and she might even seek legal culpability.

- She is ever manipulating your emotions with the aim of feeding on your pain. The extremely bizarre and sick behavior is common among almost all sorts of narcissistic mothers that their children always refer to them as emotional vampires. Sadism is one of the strategies used to feed these emotions to the children. The narcissistic mother is actively needling you about the things you are sensitive to, she keeps saying or doing things just to wound you, she engages herself in a tormenting teasing manner but shortly, you would see a smile over her lips. For example, she takes you to a 3D horrifying movie and later insults you about your childish cry, and then she would smile delightedly over your hurtful face. In many cases, you would hear the laughter in her voice as she says distressing and stressing things to you. You would then hear her gloating over how she teased you and comfortably share with other people on how it's fun to tease you which are like recruiting them to share in her amusement. She seems to enjoy her cruelties and does not have any second thought about disguising that. She makes it clear that your pain is part of her fun. More often, she comes up with offending topics and probes you about them while closely watching at your reaction.

Additionally, this mode of emotional vampirism entails both a demand that the audience suffers while seeking attention as well. Narcissistic mothers always act as a martyr who takes the form of self-pitying and wrenching. She keeps wailing and sobbing that everyone is so selfish and no one loves her and that she doesn't want to live; she wants to die. She cares less on how her manipulation affects other people which is one of the major behaviors of narcissistic people. She is capable of creating dramas in the midst of other people's tragedies showing how she is suffering.

- She is willful and selfish. A narcissistic mom will always ensure that she wins best of everything. She follows and believes in her own ways and will pursue it manipulatively and ruthlessly even if it will cost her some extra efforts or going past the normal behavior. She makes enormous efforts to win something you denied her even if you were right about her not having it or she demanded it in an unreasonable and selfish way. If you are having a party and notify her to bring her friends, she will make sure that her friends will come even if she had not planned about that. She will lie that you are the one who invited them for you to carry the burden of either giving in or making the decision to embarrass them at your doorsteps. If, for instance, she wants to come over to your house and you refuse, she chooses to call your spouse and ends up being granted the permission. However, she will not notify you and will appear as a surprise which will be a total embarrassment to you.

Moreover, since most narcissist mothers are self-centered and selfish, one of the major characteristic common with all of them is that they are bad gift-givers. They will get market things or hand-me-downs for themselves as presents for you. For example, they can give you their old bicycle as a gift and buy a new one for themselves. They believe that new things do not suit you and argue that you are a quid pro quo. However, if you surprise her with something she likes, then she will probably buy you something of your choice but she will ensure that you realize how it pains her to give you anything. As a result, she might buy you an item and get an identical item for themselves or they can choose to take you shopping, buy you a gift, and at the same time, buy something better for herself to make her feel better.

- She regularly shames her children. Narcissistic mothers always use shaming as a weapon to ensure that their children will never develop constant self-esteem or identity to make sure that they will never become independent enough to live without her approval or validation. She publicly shames her children for not achieving much personally, professionally, socially, or even academically. She shames them with regard to their preferences, personality, dressing manner, lifestyle, friends, partner, and career choices. When her children act with any sense of agency, she shames the following fear that she will lose power and control. As a consequence, she instills a sense of being not good enough regardless of their achievements.

- Narcissistic mothers are marginalized. It is weird thinking that some narcissistic mothers are threatened by their children's success, promise, and potential and confronts them negatively by challenging their self-esteem. A narcissistic mother feels threatened and as a result, she makes some effort to put down their child so that they would remain superior. Some of the examples of a marginalized narcissistic mother include rejecting the success and accomplishments of their children, unfair comparison with peers, unreasonable criticism and judgments, and nit-picking. For instance, a narcissistic mother would confront her offspring with phrases like, "you will never be good enough."

Chapter 5

The Future Of Your Relationship

The future of what your relationship will look like with your mother is ultimately going to depend on you and what you think will be the best for your situation. With that being said, I strongly advise taking a lengthy break from talking to your mom while you heal yourself from her abuse and then ease yourself back into any sort of relationship you might share if this is the path you choose. Attempting to heal from your mom's abuse while keeping yourself trapped in the cycle by maintaining a fairly close relationship, or at least a consistent relationship, during the healing cycle can disrupt your results. You might find yourself constantly getting dragged back in despite how much effort you put into healing, which can leave you feeling extremely poorly about yourself.

With narcissistic mothers there are generally three ways that the relationship can go: you can break away entirely, you can have a small relationship, or you can have a consistent relationship with strong boundaries. What you choose will depend on your chosen coping methods and the level of relationship that you can personally handle without feeling impacted by her abuse. This means that after your break you should slowly build your relationship back up and not exceed what feels right for you, to ensure you do not get sucked into old behaviors that could lead to a complete relapse in your relationship.

What to Do If Your Relationship Must End Completely

The idea that your relationship with your mother might need to end completely can be incredibly painful, especially if you have spent a large portion of your life hoping it would get better. Until this point in your life, you may have been under the influence of the belief that you could somehow contort yourself to make things better and that this would lead to your mom like you more and your relationship is fixed. Unfortunately, this is not real and there is no true hope of your relationship ever being the one that you want it to be, as hard as that is to admit. Believe me, it took me a long time and many relapses in my relationship with my mother to realize that she was never going to be the nurturing, supportive, loving mother that I wanted and needed.

If you find yourself in a position where your relationship must end completely, it might be since your mother's abuse is extreme, possibly on the brink of violent, or causing severe toxicity and trauma in your life. Your mother may be abusive to the point where you cannot have even one conversation with her without her creating a web of abuse, which leads to you feeling like you need to end the relationship completely. In this case, what you need to do is completely cut all ties and keep those ties cut. If you find yourself in a situation where the severity of the narcissism is so advanced that you must cut ties, you must remember why the situation got this advanced. When you find yourself wanting to relapse into a relationship with your mother, you must remember the reason why you no longer have a relationship with her in the first place. If you go back and forth in relationships that are this damaging it can be even more damaging as you begin to experience the trauma from your mother, as well as the trauma from yourself each time you "allow" yourself to get sucked in. This can become a huge point of guilt, and it can make healing even harder, so it is strongly advised that if you make this decision you stick to it.

What to Do If You Need to Minimize Your Relationship

In some situations, you may not need to, or maybe you can't, completely end your relationship with your mother. In this case, it is ideal that you minimize your relationship with her. Minimizing your relationship can look however you want it to look, but ultimately it requires you to avoid seeing or talking to your mother consistently. You might find yourself only talking to her when it's the holidays and you are together at a family gathering, or possibly up to once or twice a month. The frequency of this relationship ultimately depends on you and what you genuinely feel that you can handle with your mother.

This is the area where I fall with my mother. The rest of my family is quite close and I want to make sure that I maintain a relationship with them, which inevitably means that I need to be around my mother from time to time. Aside from these visits, however, I do not contact my mother because it does not feel right for me to do so. I feel stronger when I experience life on my own than I do when I attempt to celebrate with or confide in my mother only to be met with emotional unavailability and abuse. For that reason, this is my best coping method. Even with the minimal amounts of time we see and talk to each other, it still takes immense strength for me to stand strong in my coping methods and refrain from getting sucked into my mother's drama and abuse.

What to Do If You Need to Stay Consistent in Your Relationship

Some daughters will continue to have a fairly consistent relationship with their mother, even after they heal from narcissism. This is often very uncommon, however, as it can be extremely challenging to remain truly removed from the dysfunction when you are still regularly being exposed to your mother and all of her symptoms. The daughters who do find themselves capable of consistently communicating with their mothers and maintaining high-frequency relationships require massive amounts of strength to be able to uphold their boundaries and stay strong. It is incredibly challenging to break the dynamic between the mother and daughter in this scenario because the mother already has it so ingrained in her, and it is all the daughter has known since birth. In these relationships, the mother often knows exactly what to say to push the buttons of her daughter to force her back into the abuse cycle.

Due to the complexity of narcissism and the tact and calculated abuse they dish out, it is important to realize that the likelihood of you being able to maintain a consistent relationship with your mother and heal from her abuse is highly unlikely. If you do attempt to retain this type of relationship, there is a good chance that you are doing so because of her grooming and conditioning to force you to believe that it is required and that you are somehow a bad person if you don't. It may even be due to her smearing you and abusing you if you do try to stand up for yourself and get away from the abuse.

Make sure that if you are going to try this that you strongly consider why you are doing it and that if you must, you constantly work on increasing your strength and boundaries and upholding them in your relationship. You can never let your guard down here, or your mother will see the opportunity and attempt to take advantage of it. No matter how far you may get with protecting yourself, your mother will always be attempting to abuse you throughout your entire life. She will likely even go so far as to use compliance as a way to show you that the relationship can be "all better" to reel you in, just to start the dynamic all over again. You must always be cautious and in control of this relationship, no matter what. For that reason, it is likely going to be far too draining for you to uphold and it is not a good idea to aim for this type of relationship.

Chapter 6

Narcissistic Mothers And Their Sons

A relationship that a man has with his mother is as complicated just as a relationship with a daughter and her mother.

I think that what will happen is as we move forward more and more men are going to have to face what is really at the root of some of the things that they're struggling with. A narcissistic mom is someone who is not capable of attuning herself to her children, so her children are like things she owns; her property and they owe her.

A first specific area of the relationship between the male child and the narcissistic mother is her behavior with all people who have a relationship with his son.

The overt narcissistic mother is aggressive, abrasive, and intolerant. For her everybody else is an asshole, everybody else is stupid especially other women. So, it's a little bit easier to see that this person is narcissistic, but you could have narcissistic moms where it's not so easy to spot.

A covert narcissist mother can come off like she actually really cares about her son and you might not be able to witness or understand that there is a dependency that's being fostered.

In both situations (overt and covert) narcissistic mothers are using their sons for a source of supply.

There is an investment happening, there is an unconscious desire to consume the son and to create a dependency which is to always have a source of supply. So that the son never has the ability to go out and become a separate individual from her.

Narcissistic mother's agenda is to make sure that she's number one, to ensure that this young man never goes out and leaves her. So other women are considered a threat, she'll consider his friends a threat and she'll find something wrong with every person that her son brings in the house. She'll have a problem with his friends' mothers or his friends' fathers, she'll have a problem with every teacher his son has.

Another big trouble is the relationship with her husband and father of her son. Often a narcissistic mom has married a very co-dependent man. She puts him down in front of the children and makes fun of him sexually. Lots of men have witnessed how their narcissistic mothers have battered their fathers in front of them, maybe not in front of neighbors and other family members but behind closed doors definitely.

This is the kind of chaos that happens when you have a narcissistic mother and a father who is co-dependent and has been emasculated and constantly beaten down.

If you're the son of this couple, you probably have no idea how to go up against this type of a personality. You are being abandoned emotionally by this man who has just run out of steam. He goes to work, comes home to be criticized and has to sleep on the couch.

Nothing he does is ever good enough. There's always something to complain about and so you've been abandoned by this man who should be teaching you how to stand up for yourself and not be abused, but that's not happening.

On the flip side of the coin, this is your father whom your mom is putting down and you don't realize that what she's doing is really conditioning you to be afraid, to be like him.

She's trying to make sure that you feel dependent upon her and obligated to her and you have the feeling of disappointment. She's trying to find a way to make sure that you don't do to her what your dad has done to her, which is abandon her, because that's the way she sees it.

Mom needs to know that her son has put her in the center of his life. Therefore, the son of a narcissistic mother is terrified, living in a state of survival. There's also the loss of the self and this is a problem in terms of emotional development.

The young boy is not permitted to feel free enough to explore his environment without fear and so there's a lot of insecurity in the young boy who has a narcissistic mom and that carries over to adolescence when this young man wants to bring home a date.

The mom will find a problem with the date and will actually gaslight the date creating a lot of problems. The son will get the message that the mom is not happy that he brought the girl home. Statements like "That girl only wants you for your money", "That girl's gonna go out and get pregnant by you", or "You're gonna have to support her and some kid for the rest of your life" will be floated around. You could be 12 and that's the kind of crap that your mother will be telling you, so you're getting the message.

It also happens that the narcissistic mothers would always play sick the minute her son wants to go out to play baseball or tell her he has a girlfriend. Mommy would get sick and the boy would have to abandon and prove to his mother that she is number one in his life and this just gets repeated over and over.

There's a lot of fear of disappointing mom. You feel obligated to put her needs first and when you're focusing on trying to please mom, you're losing yourself. When this becomes an issue for you, you don't have the ability to connect to it, so you feel like you have low self-esteem and lack an identity.

Now when you're around other people you feel insecure, you have anxiety, but it's absolutely not your fault.

As you get older, get married and have children, your narcissistic mother will be a problem because she wants to make sure that you understand that she comes first and she wants to make sure that the women in your life and even your children know that mom comes first before everything.

Narcissistic mom will see the women in your life as competitors. Your wife will definitely feel like there's a mistress in the room and even though you are not sleeping with your mom, this energy will be a part of your life.

You will be conflicted if you're not aware that mom is a narcissist and that she's trying to control you and she wants to take center stage and she doesn't really care about any chaos she's creating in your life.

Then if you're not aware of that, you might be confused and might push your wife back because you have all these conflicts and you've been groomed since you're a little boy to worry about mommy.

You might also have tremendous fear about cutting your wife off, which is what your mom wants to do. When that happens, she has gained control over a very pretty primitive fear, which is the fear of being abandoned by the person who created you. That's like death to a new born.

You might not realize that your mother is intrusive, that she talks bad about your wife, that she has no compassion or empathy for you, nor does she have compassion or empathy for your wife. You might not recognize that mom talks bad about everybody. You might not recognize that mom has a difficult time maintaining friendships.

You might not realize that mom has to prove superior to everybody, that mom might have a drinking problem, a shopping problem, gambling problem, or that there might be some underlying addiction that you're not aware of.

And because she has primed you to fear being able to set a boundary, you as the son of a narcissistic mom may have marital problems or relationship problems with females who are feeling this heat from mom.

This tug-of-war in the mind of the son of the narcissistic mothers could be serious. They love their mother who has conditioned them to be afraid too much to let them go. Also, they are struggling with addiction or low self-esteem, or that situation where you feel like an alien in your own skin.

If you are a son of narcissistic mother, you may have tremendous cognitive dissonance. You might love and hate her at the same time. You might have tremendous rage when it comes to women because you're so angry at your mom, but you might not understand where it's coming from...and that rage is valid. This doesn't mean you abuse women or blame your girlfriend, or daughter or the cashier you know at the corner store.

What it means is that as a son of a narcissistic mother, you recognize that you have been abused. It means that you recognize that you have not been permitted to grow, develop and attune yourself to what is right. You have not been permitted to be who you are. You have had your emotions screwed with.

You have been manipulated and toyed with for this woman's agenda and the anger and the rage that you feel is valid and that's why it's important to work this out.

In psychotherapy, it's important to work this out with somebody who gets it right. It's very important that if you're going into therapy you find somebody who is well versed in narcissism, especially when it comes to be the child of a narcissist. This person should be able to allow you to express your anger and rage and to get it all out. You can work it out so that you can be more logical and rational about how you feel so that you can make decisions regarding your future.

It's not your fault if you've experienced co-dependency. Lots of men who have narcissistic mothers find themselves co-dependent. They tend to be the type of men that women walk all over, are afraid of making women angry, attract women who lie and take advantage of them.

There is also another take on this: some of these men end up with high narcissistic traits themselves. Where in some situations, mom has put her son on a pedestal and mom seems very sweet and very coddling and very nurturing and all of that, but there's almost an emotional incest that can happen and mom isn't as overt as another narcissistic mom. She's kind of passive-aggressive in her comments about women. She's passive-aggressive about being left alone but the message is "don't ever leave me, I have to come first". So, she might say things like "that girl's not good enough for you" or "she should treat you better".

But then, what happens could be like a mother-son tag-team and if you're not aware of the enmeshment and the dependency upon mom's approval and need for validation and the way she's manipulating the situation, you make sure that she's the goddess of your life forever.

If you're not aware of what's happening, if you don't know that's dysfunctional and that you have not cut the cord to mom, then when you attract a woman into your life there will be a competition and it will be you and your mother against this woman.

If you are the son of a narcissistic mother, there are so many ways this can play out. If you have an overt narcissistic mother it might be easier for you to see it and you might be able to recognize that your mother turned you against every woman you ever brought in the house and she talked bad about everybody: every man, every woman, every child.

She just infused you with the idea that the world is a scary place because she wants you to be the number one in your life to be and be sure that she always has this source of her narcissistic supply.

A healthy mother knows that it's her job to prepare her child for when she is no longer here on planet Earth. Narcissistic mothers don't care, they feel entitled to exploit you emotionally, they will guilt trip you and make you feel like you're not making the right decisions, they will create great guilt inside of you, great shame inside of you.

It will be difficult for you to make a decision without your mother, so as an adolescent she will beat you down and insinuate that you're not doing anything right. That's the overt narcissistic mother that is easier to see. If you want to do things on your own, she will find ways to gaslight you, she will find ways to insinuate that it is a stupid idea, and she will find ways to clip your wings.

As you grow up and attract females, you will have to find something wrong with every female. If you get married, your mom will be a constant source of pain for you and your wife, she will resent your children, she will resent your wife, and she will resent you.

When you tell her that something wonderful happened, she'll find a way to downgrade it. Her agenda is to get you to worry about her, if you give her any idea that she is being replaced there's going to be an issue. It is important if you're the son of a narcissistic mother, you may feel very conflicted and may have anger and rage if you are not aware of what's going on.

There are adult children of narcissistic mothers who become people-pleasers and doormats for women and they actually will attract women who are abusive towards them, because they won't know how to set boundaries. And it's just a repeat, it's like they marry their mom.

And then there are men who take on narcissistic traits, so they feel conflict with their mother. They felt controlled by their mothers, so their agenda is no woman's going to control me, no girlfriend or wife is going to control me because they're a little bit more aware of how they feel about their mother. They might even hate their mother.

They still might want a relationship with a woman and a sexual relationship even, but they might struggle with conflict because their mother was such a tyrant. There are so many ways this programming can manifest in your life, so it's important that we understand that what happened to us in our childhood because it affects us as adults.

You must understand what has happened to you as a result and you must understand the tremendous consequences that having a narcissistic mother has had.

You have been told that life is scary when it comes to getting married there's always a chance that you could get divorced and there's always a chance that you could be abandoned by a woman.

There is always a chance for abandonment issues to manifest. That's really something we need to heal from especially if we have narcissistic mothers because that fear might cause us to be emotionally avoidant and unavailable. It might cause us to be highly narcissistic because we're afraid of being abandoned.

It's so important that all of us recognize how having narcissistic parents affect us as adults and we have to heal this gaping wound inside of our hearts that has been created by this narcissistic parent.

We have a need to be vulnerable, but we're frightened, we're afraid of being engulfed and enmeshed with. We have a need to trust people, but we don't trust people. We have a need to be loved but we don't love ourselves.

This is what happens as adults and so if you are the son of a narcissistic mother, there is help. The most important thing that you can do is researching and understanding the consequences of what has happened to you.

Understand that if you've had a dad who has been beaten down by a narcissistic mother and haven't seen a man assert boundaries and as a result you don't know how to reserve boundaries with a female or with other people, it is not your fault.

It's not your fault if you have a mom who puts you on a pedestal and now, you're starting to realize that she created a dependency on you so that you would never leave her and no one, no other woman would ever replace her.

When you're starting to become aware of that, you might start to feel angry, and that's normal because your childhood was robbed from you. Your innocence and ability to feel vulnerable was robbed from you.

So, your anger is valid, but that doesn't mean now you go kick the dog or take it out on other innocent females. It means you do your work. It means you figure it out with a wonderful psychotherapist.

You might need to talk to specialists and psychotherapists that are skilled in the area of narcissistic abuse and childhood trauma and those that you feel can attune themselves to you. You have to really think about all of that before you go into therapy.

It's very important that if you're going to deal with the psychotherapist, you deal with somebody who when you interview them you feel like they have the ability to attune themselves to you because what's happened to you is that you have had your feelings completely invalidated and have been marginalized.

You have a great conflict inside of you. You have a need as a man to feel seen right. You have a need as a man to be able to express how you feel truly; feel about your mother in a safe place without being judged.

Your friends could say you shouldn't feel that way about your mother or you could have a therapist saying like you have to forgive your mother. But with the right therapist you can actually learn to set boundaries with other people and know that whether you are in a relationship with someone or not you are enough, that you have your identity, that you have a right to be happy, a right to attune yourself to your innate gifts, and you have a right to joy.

So, there is hope that those of you, those sons with narcissistic mothers, you feel heard. It's not your fault, you were raised by a narcissistic mother and the good news is you can heal. The good news is that you can reclaim your right of a healthy and happy life.

You can learn to love yourself and have healthier relationships with other women, you can attract different types of females. You absolutely must know there is hope for you.

Chapter 7

How To Deal Withnarcissistic Parents

The real trouble of narcissistic parents is that they aren't just selectively narcissistic. A lot of people will rib on their parents for being embarrassing at family get-togethers or for being naggy or needy. However, narcissistic parents far exceed the acceptable realm of embarrassing and annoying parenting to the point of being massively damaging to their child's emotional development. Narcissistic parents make one of the gravest of all parenting mistakes: caring more about themselves than their children.

One of the biggest questions you ask yourself when you've been raised by narcissists and you become sick of their mental games is how you can deal with them now that you're of age. There are a few different scenarios that we're going to look at, but they all are relatively conducive to the idea of moving past the neglectful and hurtful grasp of the narcissistic mother and/or father.

We're going to start tackling this by remembering something we've addressed several times in this book: the absolute necessity of admitting to yourself that your parents are not perfect. One of the hardest parts of moving on from abuse, in general, is to admit that there was a problem in the situation and that, unfortunately, you were not above the horrible and disgusting odds of the universe. It can happen to anyone and, sadly, it can happen to you.

I'm going to propose something absolutely unthinkable to you. Perhaps you don't need to maintain contact with your parents. In the last century, especially in the last half-century, societal attitudes toward parental relationships have changed a little bit. For one, there has started to be a lot more awareness about mental, emotional, and physical abuse. These things which normally went unquestioned or were just seen as a harsh reality of life that wasn't really talked about would eventually start to be seen as major negative forces. There is no longer a societal tolerance for violent or abusive undertones within the family structure.

On top of this, people have also started to see dropping one's parents as a realistic option in response to abusive situations. However, some cultures frown at this notion as most still place an emphasis on maintaining family ties above all else and ultimately holding an extreme reverence for your parents, whether or not they truly deserve it.

Fortunately, though, reality doesn't necessarily contend with this idea, and the notion of dropping contact with abusive parents has started to be seen as a more viable option in today's climate. While it still will get you some weird looks, each generation is increasingly accepting affected people's choice of cutting ties with their abusive or narcissistic parents.

So, in essence, the first thing that you should do to deal with narcissistic parents is to limit the effect that they can have on you as much as they can. Really, this is the best thing to do in general, so much of this chapter will focus on this aspect. The thing is that narcissism ultimately comes down to how one person expresses control over another and how they force the person to validate their image of themselves and their incredibly fragile ego. Therefore, it's not uncommon for narcissistic parents to maintain whatever means they have to express control over you. For this reason, it's important that you get to severing these as quickly as possible.

If it hasn't happened already, you should first and foremost set up a plan. If you're still living with your narcissistic parents, then set up a plan discreetly so that you can move out. There are likely options available to you. For example, if you're currently attending college, you can likely live on campus and have the college subsidize it to one extent or another, or it may even be worth taking out loans for the quality of life improvement that it will bring to you.

The next thing you have to consider is what you currently and actively depend on them for if anything. Are they your lifeline in one way or another? Are they currently handling things like your phone bill or your car insurance payment? If so, you need to incorporate these things into your plan. Estimate your personal costs for doing these on your own and incorporate them into the overall cost of living into the rent prices you're estimating.

The sad truth is that if these sorts of things exist, your parents will hold them over your head if you try to move out. They will threaten to cut them off anyway, so you might as well have a plan for when they do exactly that. If you've already moved out, or you're away for college, and they're still trying to hold some sort of unnecessary control over your life - an example might be refusing to allow you to date in college, or else they'll turn off your phone or quit paying your car payments or refuse to help you with your loan payments - then you need to still assert these things in your plan.

One obvious thing that you're going to need to do is to get a job if you don't already have one. Unfortunately, narcissistic parents often won't allow their children to get jobs because it provides them with a sense of independence and makes them less reliant upon the narcissistic parent. Therefore, you may need to couchsurf with friends until you have enough to get off your feet. If this happens, just recognize that you very well may end up being without a phone or driving without insurance for a month or two, so try to allot for these. Avoid driving if you won't have insurance and plan around the local public transit systems if there is one or try to arrange rides to and from your responsibilities from friends and coworkers.

Really, what you're essentially trying to do is to limit whatever hold that they might have over you so that they no longer have anything to hold over your head. This can be the most difficult part of this whole process, but the reality is that if you're dealing with narcissistic parents, there is very little chance that they will ever come around to realizing that they act in a narcissistic manner. In fact, the chances are pretty good that they're never going to even have the self-awareness to do so. This presents you with a very unfortunate ultimatum that you never really asked for: either you can try to limit the overall amount of interaction that you have with your parents and completely mitigate contact with them - which is the path that's conducive to becoming someday fully healed - or you must continue contact with them and risk always having that narcissistic and toxic presence in your life.

In the end, it's unfortunate, but if you really want to be afforded the opportunity to grow as a person and to start to repair some of the trauma that's occurred over the course of being raised by narcissists, you're going to most likely have to cut them off or severely limit the contact that you have with them.

The sad truth is that they are simply unable to maintain healthy relationships because they have no desire to. No amount of wishing on your end will fix this problem. Moreover, no amount of work on your end or attempts to get them to review how they act or argue them into considering why they are the way that they are is not going to go well for you. The best case is that they manipulate you into thinking that they're going to change and then experience a slow return to form as if nothing ever happened in the first place.

Well, that's not true. The best case, if your parents are narcissists, is that they'll have the ability to look inward at what happens and what causes it within themselves. If they genuinely can empathize with you and are willing to put you over themselves, then there may be some sort of headway made. You cannot, however, rely on this possibility.

Once you've taken account of all of the things that you rely on your parents for, if anything, and have a clear-cut plan along with a backup plan, you can finally start to carve out some sort of forward motion. You need to start acting on your plan and moving towards mitigating contact with your parents or cutting them off completely.

In the beginning stages of this process, they will invariably try to guilt you about what you're doing. For example, they'll say things like "Someday I'll be dead, and you'll wish you hadn't done this" or similarly manipulative things to make you feel bad about cutting them off. They may even send you hateful, threatening, or outright toxic text messages, emails, voicemails, or messages on social media. They may try to worsen your position with any family members that they're in contact with by slandering you and making things up about you.

The most important thing is that, firstly, you take the time to mentally prepare for any of the backlashes that you expect of them and that you take steps to mitigate it before it ever even has the chance to happen. Cutting off a parent or parents is one of the most difficult choices one will ever have to make, but if you want the opportunity to move forward with your life and truly start to deal with the trauma they've inflicted upon you, it may be the only proper way to deal with your narcissistic parents.

Chapter 8

Recovery

You might be wondering why most of this book is about the damage rather than the very important part of the recovery. Going back and understanding what happened is a large and very important part of the recovery. Understanding how and why you experienced your existence the way you did, and the dynamics of narcissistic manipulations, is the beginning of the healing process.

You have to take this journey for yourself, no matter how painful it might be at times. You have to find out where your behaviour patterns came from. Instead of experiencing emotions in an infantile state you'd be able to calm the child you were and take a hold of your reactions and emotions as a grown person.

This journey takes time and effort, but it's worth it. Narcissists are very unlikely to change because they are unable to see how much is wrong with them, but you can change.

Steps To Recovery

NO CONTACT

In my case, no contact was an easy choice. But if you are a young person there are other things to consider.

Going away physically is not enough and you have to be well enough to make it on your own. There was a time I was not able to get away because of depression and mental breakdowns.

If you are not in a state to cope on your own you need to recover sufficiently first. It is not impossible. Do not rush into anything. For you there are techniques you can you use to minimise the damage of living with a narcissist.

It might be even more beneficial if you can get the narcissists out of you head even when they are next to you. Remember, it is your decency, your guilt, your good nature that feeds them. If you figure out how they manipulate you, you can prevent it and even manipulate them until you can find a healthier and happier way to be.

Learn about those techniques – for example, the 'observe, do not absorb,' and the 'grey stone' technique.

Learn as much as you can about the disorder. Do not directly challenge the narcissistic parent with what you've learned. It's pointless, and it's dangerous at this stage. Resist the urge, though you might experience strong feelings of anger and hurt. Remember your target is to get better. Recovery should be your goal, not taking the narcissist down.

Once you know more by using the 'observe, do not absorb' technique, you can see through the manipulation and remain unaffected. Start understanding the reasons they behave the way they do and why you react to them the way you do.

'Grey stone' is about not feeding the narcissist with your emotions. Do not provoke them, though they will try to get the best out of you as you get better.

Do what one should do to get away from any abuser when exhausted and mentally unfit – make a realistic plan of escape, or you might make matters worse. In the meantime, keep on learning about narcissism and about techniques to improve your mental health. Do not try to explain to the flying monkeys what the narcissists are. It is your first goal to help yourself, and once you are healthy you can help others.

If You Are An Adult Child Of A Narcissist

If you are an adult child of a narcissist, then there is no question: go no contact. Do not try to explain anything to them, just get out. You have your own life, cut any contact and stay away from your dysfunctional family of origin. Nothing is worth the mental destruction they cause. They will end up worse off, and you have everything to gain.

The point I am trying to make is that if you are unable to relax when you are with your family of origin, if you feel miserable because of them, then you don't have to stay. You've been conditioned not to believe your feelings. But if you feel bad when you are with certain people, they are not good for you. If you can avoid it, do not force yourself to be near them out of any false sense of duty or fear.

I cannot repeat it enough: do not explain yourself to the narcissistic parent. There is no point of getting into any verbal arguments. They flourish in it, and you will suffer. Don't fight them directly. They will play the victim, and they are expert manipulators able to feed on any attention, as long as they are in some way still involved in your life.

As long as they have an access they will feed on your emotions. If you have to talk to them, stay distant and do not give them information about yourself. Just say you do not wish to have any contact with them, and that's that.

A win against a narcissist is living a good life.

You have to learn to stick with your truth whether others believe you or not. Covert narcissists are not obvious to most people. Start the healing process and work on a new way of thinking and feeling about yourself.

You are going to meet other narcissists, do not let them in your life. And if you do, you have to employ the 'grey stone' and the 'observe but do not absorb' techniques, and try to get rid of them.

Most importantly, forgive yourself for any mistakes you have made in the past. You survived, and you were under attack ever since you were born. It takes someone with ability, sense, and intuition. Embrace who you are, even when you feel fragile and exhausted.

Forgiveness is often used in a religious sense – forgive those who have wronged you. This is not what I mean. Victims of narcissistic abuse tend to punish themselves for being stupid and not figuring out sooner what the narcissistic game was. This is just a repeat of a bad pattern of thinking. It was never your fault, but forgiving is about letting go and moving on. Embrace and respect yourself.

Do Not Believe Narcissists Will Change

Once you get away, the narcissistic parent will try to get you back with all sorts of pretences. Don't fall for it, not again. Your toxic family has roles, and everything they do is to push you back into the Scapegoat role. Do not give them any information about yourself and do not try to explain anything.

Other Things To Know About No Contact

As I mentioned before, physically getting away from the narcissists will not heal you alone. No matter how far you go, their poison is inside you. It is just the first step, then you have to go through a healing process. If you come from a narcissistic family you have to rethink the entire value system instilled in you and stop feeling inferior.

And as you break free from the narcissistic illusion and your dysfunctional family, you will experience a lot of hatred coming at you from the narcissistic parent and their flying monkeys. And you will be unfairly judged by people not close enough to know what the real story is. You have to get through it and learn to stay with your truth.

Yes, I know how deep the childhood desire to please is. But think about it: If you are liked by a narcissist, you have to worry. If they hate you, it's because you are doing well and you are no longer playing their sick games.

The same is true of the flying monkeys: they are not worth your time. Move on. Even from close relatives - it is not your job to save them from the narcissist. First of all you have to save yourself.

You have to accept that not all people are good, and not all mothers are good. Most are, and mothers are very important, and this is why the few unlucky ones have to deal with a world of pain.

Beginning The Healing Process

There are things to keep in mind and things to avoid.

Going back to the earliest memories and reviewing them is a good place to start. It's where your brain will not want to go to at first, but it is a necessary part of the process.

Once you start understanding the damage the childhood abuse did, you are going to feel an overwhelming anger. Be angry, but do not act on it. You will not be in a state to make sound decisions about what to do. Remember, your anger will subside with time.

Do not be afraid to feel your emotions, as long as they don't control you. Be honest and try to verbalise what you feel, because you've been made to ignore your senses and your needs. When you experience overwhelming feelings, put your hand on your chest and say aloud how you feel. This works for anger, and for any other strong emotion. Just saying what you feel reduces it by half.

You have to go through a grieving process, grieving the loss of time and the loss of the hope that you will ever have good, supportive parents. Go through the stages without holding back, till you are ready to let go.

Don't break no contact. Learn techniques to improve your daily life and to combat stress and Complex PTSD.

Love yourself unconditionally, because you are going to make the old mistakes a few more times. It's easy to fall into the old pattern of behaviour when you are stressed and tired. Be very kind and patient with yourself when you do, try to calm the little child inside. Your reactions to your mistakes will make the real difference in time.

As a rule, do not try to explain to people who have never experienced narcissistic abuse. They have to experience it, or be very fine-tuned emotionally, to understand your pain. Other empaths, or people with similar experiences, will understand, and finding a community online to share with is the best thing you can do.

Someone who has never been a victim and is reading this might say that the narcissists are as much victims as the people they destroy, because they had some sort of abnormal childhood. They are entitled to their opinion, but not to telling you how to handle your situation.

If you are a victim of a narcissistic parent, for you and me, there are different rules. Do not ever feel sorry for a narcissist. We have our own disorder, and it makes us a prey for predatory types and users. We are who they are after, because the narcissists cannot take from a normal person as much as they can from us.

How To Handle The Inner Critic

The inner critic is the criticising voice inside your head shaped by the attitude of the narcissistic parent. Once you understand how damaging it is you can change it by catching it as it tries to put you down and consciously changing the message to a positive and caring one.

Be patient. The inner voice was formed in your juvenile years and came with the narcissistic inbuilt position of control. It is formed with the toxic shame to work against you for the benefit of the parent.

To get into the habit and develop a positive inner voice, you have to practice saying positive things to yourself. Develop a mantra that works for you and repeat it when you get stressed.

Try to learn to love all those flaws you used to punish yourself for, love your body as it is. It will take time, but once you manage to shift your mindset you will experience enormous relief and a sense of freedom.

Emotional Flashbacks

You might have never heard of emotional flashbacks, but as a child of a narcissist you are more than likely to have experienced them.

Those are flashbacks of shaming and humiliating moments of your past. They can pop up in your head at any time and make your mind re-experience them. From embarrassing moments at school, to traffic mishaps, to social blunders. All those times you failed to perform are coming back in a flash, and that does nothing but feed the toxic shame.

It is something the old part of the brain does, and it's looking for danger. This is why it keeps on replaying those moments you found so distressing again and again.

When you have an emotional flashback, the muscles contract, the breathing becomes shallow, the heart beats faster, and it feels like a sharp burn in the mind and makes you flinch and retreat both mentally and physically.

Some memories are stored in a childlike state, as they were experienced. Others trigger the state of toxic shame that is imbedded in the people-pleaser's mind. Being humiliated is registered as danger in your mind, because it was in the narcissistic family.

Dealing With Emotional Flashbacks

To combat their effect, learn to recognise emotional flashbacks and acknowledge that you are having a flashback.

Then take a deep breath and bring yourself to the present. Say 'I am having a flashback' aloud if you need to. Put your hand on your chest. Remember you are safe and well now, and that you have a choice how to feel. Those flashbacks are useless and harmful, and they are the result of dysfunction and self-hatred.

Relax your body and be very compassionate to yourself. Consciously examine where it came from, and try to point to the underlying issues triggering the wave of toxic shame.

Without the toxic shame, the flashbacks are just human experiences, and everybody has experiences like that. You are not supposed to be perfect or better than everyone to matter, this was the poison of the narcissistic abuser who shamed you out of your mind. Be compassionate and very nice to yourself.

Eventually, you will move your reaction to the frontal lobe, rethink the danger and react with reason rather than with emotion and fear.

Chapter 9

Healing From Narcissism

The effect of emotional and physical neglect from a narcissistic mother can be disastrous if you don't find a way out.

Before you even try to recover from the wounds, you need first to notice that you have a wound to heal and that the wound was caused by the abuse from your mother.

Here are signs that you have a wound to heal:

1. You Can't Overcome Perfectionism

You have the need to do more and more than is healthy and appropriate, or necessary. This means you have the drive to be perfect all the time, even in situations when you just need to be average. This is usually a strategy to cope and survive and is aimed at making you survive and get the reaction you yearn for.

The perfectionist attitude s all about the skills that you have gleaned from your parents, that if you aren't perfect, you won't serve in the family.

The bad thing is that many people teach their children that good parenting is all about pushing their kids to be excellent in all they do.

2. You Can't Say No

You are terrified at the aspect of saying no, even when you know that you don't have the capacity to do something. You know that if you negate what the parent wants, you will be faced with a lot of ridicule and shame. The parents will even go ahead and abandon them just because they have let them down.

3. You Set The Bar Too High for any Task

Accomplishments need to be measurable and easy to handle. If you find yourself achieving something but you feel like you want to take it a notch higher, then you need to get some help.

4. You Feel Like Your Mother

If you say some words and you remember what your mother said some time back, and then you are just like her, you need to get out of the loop. When you grow up in a narcissist abusive relationship with your mother, the behaviors usually rub off you, and you will find yourself behaving like her all the time.

5. You Reject Challenges

If someone has the guts to challenge you, you always make clear that you don't want it or the people don't respect you at all. You start disliking them and rejecting their advances excessively. This means you don't tolerate any competition from anyone.

The Emotional Journey To Healing

Before you can take up the healing process, you will go through various stages of grief that will dictate how things work out for you. Here are the stages.

- Acceptance

You have first to accept that your parent was a narcissist. You have to look back and then know that the parent had limited love and empathy to offer you, and this is why you became the person you are today. This means you realize that there is a problem that needs to be handled before you can heal.

- Denial

Here, you deny that the mother you loved so much wasn't capable of the love that you needed. Remember that as a child, you yearn for the love to survive, which means that if you deny this, then you can start looking at things in a totally different way.

- Bargaining

You have to realize that you have been bargaining with the narcissist mother the whole of your life, both internally and externally. You have been hoping and wishing that the mother could change for the better, but it hasn't worked the way you wanted. You have tried so many things over the years to get back their approval and love with no avail.

- Anger

Once you realize that you have been hurting for so long, you will become angry and upset. You now realize that your emotional needs weren't met by the person you trusted the most and that if things had gone the other way round, you would have been a better person.

You will feel angry at your mother for taking you through a hard time, and you will be angry at yourself for allowing your mother to take advantage of your young mind.

- Depression

This is the point when you feel intense sadness because you have realized that this isn't the kind of parent you wanted, yet you had nothing to do with it. You get resigned to the fact that your mother will never be as loving as you expect her to be. You let go of any expectations you have had for years and then grieve the loss of the vision.

When you go through these stages, you will realize that you bounce from one stage to the other, and if you find that you aren't accepting the fact, you need to go back and try the stage again. This is the only proper way to grieve. Don't go to the recovery stage until you have gone through these stages, and you have accepted that your parent had a limitation. To make it work better, try and journal the feelings you experience. Talk to your loved ones and take care of yourself throughout the whole process.

The Solutions To Healing

Let us look at the various solutions you need to follow so that you heal your body and mind from narcissistic abuse from a mother.

1. Develop Self Compassion

It might be a huge challenge for some people to develop self-compassion. This is because it might trigger some emotional memories for the people that have been exposed to abuse where compassion was used as a setup for the attack. This can also prove difficult if you grew up in an emotionally neglectful home or never received any compassion.

Developing compassion is a huge deal because, in many homes, compassion might be lacking in some areas. The kid might grow up knowing that compassion isn't something that needs to be part of their lives.

To develop compassion, try to be patient so that you can have that kindheartedness toward yourself. Try to understand what you will say to someone else in a similar circumstance, or what the actions of a friend have helped you in the past.

2.　　Remove Your Inner shame

Your inner child is always hoping that it will become smart, talented, and helpful, but you don't have to will to hack it. You will keep on trying to win the approval of the parent, which in turn makes you self-criticize yourself.

Because of the constant talks about failure in your circles, you will have an inner child that is hurt and confused. It will keep on critiquing anything you say or do.

Eliminate the shame by trying to be vulnerable to the people around you. As you begin to create connections and develop bonds with the people close to you, you will open up, and things will be better.

3.　　Learn to Trust Yourself

Try to learn to trust your decisions, opinions, and other aspects that make you a human being. Start treating yourself well because the people that are close to you will not treat you the way you want to be treated. Since you have been in an abusive relationship with a mother, you might end up missing out on the role if proper nurturing.

When you learn to trust yourself, you will be able to trust others as well. You will be able to talk to people the right way and develop the right kind of relationship with them.

Stop rejecting yourself and seek to repair the damage that a parent caused.

4. Take Care of Yourself

The parent with NPD has made sure you only focus on them and ignore what you can do to yourself. This means you will be conditioned to focus on the external part and then avoid looking deep into yourself. At the end of it all, you will find that you neglect your emotional and physical needs, which in turn leads to failure.

Start the journey towards self-care. Have that inner peace that will make you change your life for the better. Have a list of happy things that you want to do each day to change your outlook towards life.

5. Educate Yourself

Once you realize that your mother was suffering from NPD, try and learn about the condition so that you know what you are dealing with.

Image: learn about the topic

Knowledge is power, and when you have good information from chat forums, blogs, and books, you will be able to handle the process much better. With the right kind of support, you will understand what you have gone through and what you need to do to heal.

6.   Know Your Past Role

You need to understand what kind of role you played in your mother's fantasy. Were you the golden child or were you the scapegoat? All you need to understand is that you have been part of a plot that was orchestrated by your mother, and you need to find a way out as soon as possible.

Once you know your role, you need to work with the other siblings to create a unified front against her. When all of the family members understand what is going on, and they come up with the right strategy, they will be able to handle the situation much better compared to going at it alone.

If you don't trust your other siblings or you aren't united, you will have to find a way to shut down the other members and protect yourself in the process of recovery.

7.   Have Boundaries

Narcissist mothers don't recognize any boundaries that you set for them. They see you and the rest of the family as an extension of them to control and manipulate them. Whether you were the scapegoat or the golden child, you need to come up with boundaries and assert them.

Come up with healthy boundaries and make sure they are respected by the mother and other family members.

8.   Stop Blaming Yourself

If you have been the scapegoat, you always tend to blame yourself when something goes wrong. You should stop feeling guilty for the things that are beyond your control. Instead, try and find a way to stop blaming yourself and assert your authority.

Chapter 10

How Manipulations Influence Your Mindset

Manipulation is one of the main tactics a narcissistic mother will use to control and influence their daughter's mindset. Whether their daughter is an adult or a child growing up, mothers apply various tactics aimed at asserting their control and authority on their daughters.

Here, we discuss various harmful manipulation tactics, what the mother aims at achieving, and how you can identify and overcome them as a daughter.

Tactics Narcissist Mothers Use To Manipulate Their Daughters And Overpower Them

Children who were brought up by narcissistic parents have gone through a lifetime of abuse. A narcissistic mother lacks empathy and exploits her daughter for her agenda. In most cases, this mother refuses to undergo treatment to move from her destructive behavior.

They expose their children to psychological mistreatment as they bully, manipulate, coerce, control, and terrorize them. The children of narcissistic parents are so traumatized, and they are placed at risk of suicide, depression, anxiety, low self-esteem, substance abuse, and attachment disorders.

Should a daughter of a narcissist mother stay in contact with her mother, even as a grown-up, she would continue to experience the same abuse and manipulation in her adulthood. However, as an adult, you can break away. You can seek treatment, reduce contact with your mother, and seek alternative coping methods.

A narcissistic mother uses different manipulation tactics to control and influence the mindset of her daughter. Here, we discuss the different tactics a narcissistic mother will use on her daughter and tips on coping mechanisms and safe-care for the daughter.

Emotional blackmail

A narcissistic mother has mastered the art of demanding from her daughter in the form of a request. Should the daughter say no or request for time to think through it, the mother puts pressure on her and threatens ugly consequences. If the daughter stands her ground and refuses, she will punish her daughter through silent treatment, sulking, withholding important things, sabotage, and, in some cases, violence.

For instance: Your narcissistic mother may call to tell you that she is coming over for a visit, but because you know her abusive ways and your schedule doesn't allow for visiting, you decline her request. Instead of respecting your wishes, your mother will begin talking about how she took care of you, how you are ungrateful, how she sacrificed a lot to see you where you are, but, now, you have no time for her. At this point, she doesn't care what your reasons are but will disconnect the phone and decide not to talk to you for weeks.

How to cope: You must know you are within your rights to say no and protect your boundaries. You have a right to protect yourself from your narcissistic mother's abusive ways and your family members, as well. Don't give in to her manipulations; allow her to sulk or go silent, and when she is ready, she will reach out. Do not, at any time, allow yourself to discuss your decision, and if she leaves manipulative messages, ignore them until she realizes on her own that she needs to respect your space.

Guilt-tripping

Many narcissistic parents use fear, obligation, and guilt to manipulate their children. This is also what a narcissistic mother will use on her daughter. She invokes guilt in you so that you do whatever she is asking for her good, disregarding your personal needs.

For instance: Your narcissistic mother constantly reminds you that you are getting older but without a husband child. She reminds you constantly that you have an obligation to give her grandchildren. If you dare tell her marriage is not your priority as long as you are happy, she is likely to lash out at you, condemning you for wanting her to die without grandchildren. She tells you that if you cared about her, you would have children. She tells you that all her life, she sacrificed to see you have a family, but you refuse to give her grandchildren. She tells you that it is a shame and a disgrace that you are not married at your age and, worse, you have no children.

How to cope: With this kind of talk, you are likely to feel guilty. Be aware of these feelings and discard them. Evaluate yourself and ask yourself if you have anything to feel guilty and ashamed of. Remember, you have not inflicted any pain or harm to them. You are free to live your life as you please, as long as you are not hurting another person. You have a right to your choices. They may not please your mother, but they are your choices, and you must own them. Live your life on your terms.

Shaming

A narcissistic, toxic mother uses shame to manipulate her daughter. She would demean and belittle her privately and in public. She knows your weakness and uses it to bring you down. This is a very effective manipulation tool. Using the flaws of her daughter to shame her heightens her daughter's insecurities, and for her to cope, she agrees to do whatever the mother asks so that she is not reminded of her flaws.

For Instance: You are having a family gathering, and in the middle of having fun and interacting with other members, your mother picks on you to discuss your weight issues. You may be successful, but that is not enough. She shames you in front of everyone on how you don't know how to take care of yourself, and you will end up dying because of your weight. You know you are overweight, and you have struggled with this for long, but she doesn't care how you feel. She says you are bringing shame to her by looking like a balloon and not being a good role model to your kids.

How to cope: When your mother begins to shame you this way, acknowledge the emotional pain it brings you. If you feel you are becoming powerless under her attack, try your best to remove yourself from that situation and get your power back. Under no circumstances, should you let her shaming tactics work on you. Let her know she cannot shame you anymore, and tell her that if she continues, then you have no reason to see each other again. Remind her you are proud of yourself, and you have nothing to be ashamed of.

Comparison and triangulation

A narcissistic mother likes to compare her daughter with the daughters of other people to keep diminishing them. She wants her daughter to fight for her approval and attention constantly by making her feel she is not good enough. She wants her daughter to form the mentality that others are better than her.

For instance: Your mother calls you to tell you that your neighbor's daughter just made partner in her law firm, and she is getting married. She then adds a remark, asking what are you doing with your life and when are you going to make her proud.

How to cope: Do not allow her petty comparisons stress you. Remember that you are running your race at your speed and doing what makes you happy. Know that she is trying to undermine you. Change the subject or cut short the conversation. Tell her you do not appreciate her comparison and that you are happy for what your neighbor has achieved. Do not allow yourself to get into an argument with her because it will just frustrate you.

Gaslighting

This is one of the most common manipulating tactics mothers use against their daughters, as mentioned earlier. With this tactic, a toxic mother distorts reality and denies any form of abuse if you call her out. With this, she will make you feel you are the narcissistic one for even thinking it.

For Instance: Your mother calls to leave an abusive message for you and even more missed calls. This is because you were unable to do something for her. She decides to keep punishing you for it, and when you confront her regarding it, she downplays it, saying that you are making a big deal out of nothing. She would say she only made one call, and her message was not abusive. She makes you feel like you are the crazy one, and you imagined all that.

How to Cope: If your mother used this tactic often when you were a child, chances are, you suffer from self-doubt. Do not give in to this manipulation; instead, notice when your narcissistic mother's false claims don't match with reality. When you suspect a situation to be abusive, note it down, and seek help with a therapist to identify the problem. Go back and evaluate other gaslighting incidences with your mother, and see them for what they are and not what she tells you they are. Do not cover it up to cope.

Third-party reinforcements

When a narcissistic mother notices her daughter is gaining independence and cannot easily be manipulated, she takes her manipulation further by looking for reinforcement. She will convince a friend that you have a problem and confront you in her presence. When the friend supports your mother, you begin to doubt yourself, and guilt begins to build up. In the end, you end up doing what she wanted despite your own needs.

For instance: When you start working, your mother may ask you for money. If you tell her you don't have any, she might say how she had nothing when you were growing up. She would even ask her friend if she remembers how she had to do three jobs and go without sleep so that her daughter can be happy. With her friend's reinforcement, you begin to ask yourself if you are unfair to her.

How to cope: Be alert on all the tactics your mother will use. If you know you genuinely did not have extra to give her, do not allow her to manipulate you this way. You can only give money if you have extra and out of a willing heart, not out of manipulations. Keep in mind that it was her obligation to provide for you as a child, and she cannot use that to manipulate you.

Becoming a victim

A narcissistic mother will always want to play the victim, even though she is manipulating you. You may tell your mother that you feel she doesn't understand you or empathize with your feelings. Instead of listening, she will turn it around and blame you by saying she has done everything to make you feel appreciated, but you can't get enough. She'll tell you that she goes out of her way to listen and advise you, but you do not listen.

For instance: You try to tell her that you do not appreciate how she uses your flaws to shame you, both in private and in public. Instead of her hearing that, she turns it around to say she has been trying to get you to see how you can improve yourself, but you complain instead. She may say all she wants is your happiness, and no matter what she does, you seem not to see that she means well.

How to cope: Always remember your feelings are valid. See the manipulation for what it is. Shaming a person is not helping. If she wants help, she can ask you how she needs it and walks you through what she is going through, but when she criticizes you and shames you, refuse to be manipulated. Be aware when you start thinking that you had hurt her when it was you who was hurt. See the manipulation for what it is, and refuse to be pushed further.

With these signs, it is easier for you to identify and understand the various ways your narcissistic mother will manipulate you, and you can resist the manipulation. Taking to a therapist is also a good way to cope with the effects of manipulation. Do not keep quiet on the manipulation. When you notice it, call it out and avoid getting intimidated in any way. Always remember, you are the victim, and if you are feeling it, then there is something there.

Why Is Your Mother Narcissistic?

Your mother is a narcissist, not because she was born as one but because she was conditioned to become one. Children of narcissistic parents often grow up to be narcissists themselves if they do not realize it and break the cycle. Your mother may have been raised by narcissistic parents and knew that as a way of life.

Narcissism, according to psychologists, is a result of childhood experiences. An adult went through developmental states as a toddler, and their experiences shape who they are now, how they relate to their children, and how they see the world.

Toddlers who suffer neglect or overindulgence from their parents will grow up with this same perception of life.

When a child is indulged in everything as a toddler, they grow up without knowing and respecting boundaries and end up being narcissists. Because of their upbringing, they grow up believing the world revolves around them. The same signs found in narcissistic mother could be the same signs her parents showed her.

Here, we discuss why your mother has certain traits and how she developed them into narcissistic behaviors.

I. Why does your mother feel superior and entitled?

Superiority complex and entitlement is a major trait in narcissistic mothers. This trait is developed from childhood. There are a few factors that may have contributed to your mother having these traits. If your mother was raised by parents who were overindulging her and giving her everything she wanted, chances are, she developed the feeling that she was entitled to have everything, regardless of the cost. Her parents probably made her feel she was more important than anyone else, so she developed the same attitude. However, it is also possible that your mother was neglected as a child and to compensate for that, she demands attention and wants everyone to realize she is superior. Her aim is not to be ignored, and she has the power to do that to her children because the same was done to her.

II. Why does your mother need validation and attention?

If your mother was raised by parents who constantly demeaned her and told her she was not good enough, she would grow up believing she is incapable of doing anything right or achieving anything. In everything that she does, she will want to be validated that she did well because her confidence is fragile and suffers from low self-esteem from her upbringing.

On the other hand, if she was neglected and denied attention as she was growing up, she lives with the constant fear of being rejected and abandoned. She will manipulate her daughter into getting the attention she missed growing up because she feels she deserves it. She will do things, not out of the goodness of her heart, but to be praised and for people to see that she is important.

III. Why is your mother a perfectionist?

Growing up being told that she was good for nothing, and being compared to others can adversely affect a child. She grows up believing to receive love; she must be perfect. This demand put on her at an early age is detrimental and results in her never finding satisfaction in anything. She will constantly complain, and as a result, she will also expect the same from her daughter, so she will fault in everything that she does.

IV. Why is your mother so controlling?

The need to control is a narcissistic behavior common among narcissist mothers. This is derived from their need for perfection according to their standards. It feels logical for them to be in control because of their sense of entitlement. When they were growing up, their mothers ran their lives, so why not do the same to their daughters? They like being in control because it makes them feel important and needed. To them, being in control affirms their authority. In their minds, they believe a mother knows best because their mother told them the same thing.

V. Why can't your mother accept responsibility?

A narcissist like being in control, but they never take responsibility for their actions. If something goes wrong, they will apportion blame and claim it is your fault because according to them, you never followed instructions. According to her, her methods are perfect, and nothing goes wrong when she is in control.

If she was raised by a mother who always found fault in her, she will, by extension, find fault in others but never in herself. If they are found on the wrong side of the law; she is not to blame but the police officer. In most cases, she finds power in blaming those who are loyal and close to her emotionally to maintain the façade of perfectionism and control. It is easier for them to blame those close to them because they know you are not likely to leave her, but she has no hold on other people.

VI. Why can't your mother respect boundaries?

A narcissist is selfish and has an inflated sense of self. She knows where the boundaries are, but she ignores them. To her daughter, she feels you are a continuation of herself, so everything about you belongs to her, too.

It is possible that when she was growing up, her mother invaded her privacy and made friendships with her friends. A narcissistic mother will want to socialize with your friends because she wants everything that you have. It is possible that she was never taught boundaries while growing up, and in the same case, she does not respect boundaries with anyone, let alone her daughter. Should you point it out, she will find ways to manipulate you to accepting her invasion.

VII. Why can't your mother empathize with your situation?

A narcissist is naturally self-absorbed. No one empathized with her growing up, so she doesn't understand why other people's feelings should concern her. A narcissistic mother doesn't apologize, feel remorse, or feel any guilt.

As she grew up, she knew how to suppress her feelings and realize they were a burden as a child, and she expects the same in her daughter. In contrast, she understands anger, rejection, and threats because she experienced them as well. A narcissist doesn't understand sarcasm. She perceives it as agreeing with what she is saying. She does not understand how to relate to another person's feelings because she was taught how to suppress them, and a show of feelings was a show of weakness.

VIII. Why doesn't your mother understand the logic except her emotions?

Using logic to explain to a narcissist how their behavior affects or hurts you is a waste of time. She may say that she understands, but truthfully, she doesn't. She is only aware of her own emotions and feelings. If a mother had narcissistic parents, she only knew how to be manipulated emotionally but not how to discuss things using logic.

IX. Why does your mother have a splitting personality?

This is a common trait among narcissists. They can be extremely good or bad in character and also in how they view relationships. They don't accept responsibility for anything bad but are quick to take credit for all the good things.

A narcissistic mother was raised under similar circumstances. She believed the child was to blame for every bad thing, but if the child did well, it was because of her. They think of situations as either good or bad. She is unable to remember any positive things in a person, only the mistakes a person makes.

X. Why is your mother so afraid?

Most narcissists have buried fears. They grew up being demeaned, ridiculed, and rejected. Their life revolves around the fear of these things. A mother will want to control her daughter all the time to remain relevant. She is afraid of the daughter being independent because it will mean the daughter can leave them. To her, a daughter being independent is not a good thing because it means abandonment and rejection.

If a mother was rejected and neglected as a toddler, she would always be afraid of being left. She wants to control everything and the lives of her children so that they don't leave her.

On the other hand, a narcissist is afraid of true intimacy. They are afraid that others will discover her weaknesses and imperfections that she knows she has but hides from others. They are afraid to be judged and criticized because it means they are imperfect.

XI. Why is your mother anxious?

Anxiety is a condition present among most narcissists. Your mother is always afraid something wrong is about to happen. She is likely to accuse her daughter of mental illness or being selfish if she doesn't follow her wishes. She grew up being told if she did not do something, something bad was going to happen. She expects negative consequences for every action and is always looking for ways to divert it.

XII. Why is your mother ashamed of you?

A narcissistic mother harbors shame. She doesn't feel guilty because she believes she is perfect and always right but shames you at any given opportunity. The truth is she is also ashamed. She feels there is something wrong with her and cover it up. She shames you to apportion blame for what she feels deep inside of her.

XIII. Why can't my mother be vulnerable?

A narcissistic mother is unable to understand feelings. She lacks empathy and needs to protect herself from hurt constantly. Because of her upbringing, she is unable to view the world from the perspective of another person. Your mother is unable to be vulnerable because she is blind emotionally and feels lonely but covers it up. Instead of showing vulnerability, she will jump from one relationship to the next. She desperately desires for someone to see and understand her pain, but she fears to be seen weak. To hide, they are unable to relate to the feelings of others.

XIV. Why can't my mother be able to communicate well and cope with others?

Communication requires thoughtfulness, and cooperation with others requires a real understanding of other people's feelings. If a person cannot empathize, it is impossible to communicate effectively, as well as be part of a team or cope with others.

A narcissistic mother can completely alter how their daughter thinks and perceives things. Through manipulations, a mother can control her daughter so that she will never be independent. Knowing the different tactics a mother would use to manipulate and control you gives you the power to overcome and strive to establish a healthy relationship with her and with others.

Maybe you have always wondered why your mother behaves the way she does. Understanding where the narcissistic traits originate and understanding how they affect her may be the beginning of healing. It is important to understand the narcissistic personality disorder, not to condemn her but to help her overcome her ways, deal with her insecurities, and develop better relationships.

Chapter 11

Therapy

In this final chapter, we're going to get into all the reasons you should go for therapy. There's nothing but benefits when it comes to therapy, especially as a survivor of a narcissistic mother. Let's begin!

Why Therapy Is Awesome for You

You should see a mental health professional because they are in the best position to help you deal with the pain and trauma from your past relationship with your narcissistic mother. A therapist can also help you come up with the perfect coping mechanisms for you, which will be of immense help when you feel the blues coming on.

A therapist will provide a safe space for you to just let it all out. You can talk freely about how you feel without feeling like you're being judged. Even better, the therapist will help you work out the messy, mixed bag of emotions that have you terribly out of sorts.

Dealing with Depression

Depression is no joke, and as the child of a narcissistic mother, you are unfortunately prone to it. Depression is not sadness. It's more. It's like a dark cloud hovering over you. Everyone sees the sun, but all you see is darkness. You can't sleep right, you don't eat right, you're bogged down by guilt, and shame, and you're wondering if you should even be breathing right now.

Sound familiar? Do not worry. Just see a therapist. The therapist can provide you with the best treatment modality for you, help you heal, and grow past your past. They'll also help you to come up with better ways of reacting to things as they come up, as well as better ways to think about all you have been through with your mother.

Dealing with Anxiety

If there's one thing that children of narcissistic parents are not strangers to, it's anxiety. When you engage the services of a certified psychotherapist, they can help you find your center again, by figuring out exactly what situations trigger your anxiety, and then coming up with ways to handle it. They will help you understand why you feel the way you do, and help you move past the anxiety to a tranquil life.

Dealing with Obsessive Thoughts

You might find it's a battle in your mind when you try to drown out the negative stuff your narcissistic mother has programmed you to believe. You might struggle hard with quieting her voice in your head. Besides this, thoughts about going back to her, among other things can simply refuse to go away. It can be so persistent that you even begin to have dreams about it.

A psychotherapist is your best bet for dealing with these irrationally compulsive thoughts you have. They'll be able to help you dig into the root causes of these thoughts, so you can finally break their hold on you once and for all. In addition to that, your therapist can help you out with better feeling thoughts you can use instead, as well as techniques to quiet your mind and be at ease with yourself.

Helping You with Your Relationships

Because of the harm your narcissistic mother has done you, you might find you're having trouble with your relationships and friendships, either on account of her smear campaigns, or on account of you sabotaging yourself by seeking out relationships and friendships just like the one you had with good old mom. A therapist will help you learn to find and build healthier ones, and show you how to keep them thriving.

Helping You with Your Career

If you find yourself flailing in your career because of your mother, or you're not even sure which career decisions to make because you doubt yourself, there's no one better than a therapist to help you out.

You Deserve to Be Supported

Don't think you don't deserve the attention and support of a therapist. You deserve to have a life that is rich, unhampered by your past with your mother. You deserve to live your life to the fullest. You deserve to be healed. So, please see a therapist. Get the help you deserve, now.

Conclusion

Congratulations on getting to the end of this eBook. This book has been specifically written for you, as a daughter dealing with a narcissistic mother, and as a parent, trying to understand themselves. You may have been struggling emotionally for many years with your relationship with your mother. You felt that something has been wrong, and you need to find a solution. Your life has been a series of painful memories and episodes, and you want to make it right.

After reading this book, it is time to take control of your life. You have lived under the control and manipulation of your mother; you are probably doing it to your daughter, and all your relationships are affected. It is time to end the cycle of narcissism in your family. With the information you have received by reading this book, you can now identify how you relate to your mother or daughter or even your grandchild. It may also help you understand how you relate to other people. This knowledge is going to help you seek help to stop the pain from affecting your lives and forge healthier relationships, moving on.

The book has also given insights to understand that if your mother manipulated and controlled you, she did not always do it intentionally but was suffering from a narcissistic personality disorder. When you know the root cause of the behavior, together, you can seek treatment as a family and forgive one another.

This book also helps mothers check on their behaviors to control how they behave. It is possible that you have been displaying narcissistic tendencies toward your children but never realized it. Through the knowledge in this book, you can easily identify and work on any narcissistic behavior before it escalates and damages your child.

Embrace the lessons outlined here, strive to heal, and look forward to fulfilling healthy relationship with your mother, daughter, children, and partner.

Well, my friend, we've come a long way. I believe we've covered a whole lot on narcissistic mothers, and by this point, you should now know without a shadow of a doubt that you were right to pick this book up. It is my sincere hope that I've been able to open your eyes so that you can see your narcissistic mother for who she really is.

Now you know what she is, and you know what to do to free yourself of her clutches, heal, and move on with your life. However, knowing is only half the battle. Are you ready to act? Are you afraid? If you are afraid, it is understandable. It's also all the more reason you need to pull the trigger without thinking.

Speaking for myself, all the magical, wonderful relationships and experiences I have had in my life happened as soon as I cut off my narcissistic family. You read that right. Family. Seven kids, two parents. That's a whole other book right there. The point is I do know for a fact that there's nothing like the freedom and relief you feel, once you have worked through all the yucky emotions.

There are times when you might want to go back to her. I get it. But for once in your life, you have got to put you first. Not just for your sake, but for the sake of the kids you'll have, or the partner you'll spend your life with, or the good people who will come to meet in life. It would be awesome if you put yourself at the top of this list - for once.

You can heal. Are you ready to? Then seek professional help, and do what needs to be done. All survivors of narcissistic parenting will be rooting for you. You've got this. I hope that one day soon, you will be sharing your own story of freedom, and because of your story, other daughters and sons who are suffering because of their narcissistic parents will have the courage to walk away and claim their lives back.

www.ingramcontent.com/pod-product-compliance
Lightning Source LLC
Chambersburg PA
CBHW071857070526
44583CB00016B/1733